# JUST DEWEY

# JUST DEWEY

A Journey from Poverty to Creative Genius

Tom L. Arnold

LUMINARE PRESS
WWW.LUMINAREPRESS.COM

Just Dewey: A Journey from Poverty to Creative Genius
Copyright © 2024 by Tom L. Arnold

All rights reserved. This book or any portion thereof may not be reproduced or used in any manner whatsoever without the express written permission of the publisher, except for the use of brief quotations in a book review.

Printed in the United States of America

Luminare Press
442 Charnelton St.
Eugene, OR 97401
www.luminarepress.com

LCCN: 2024909942
ISBN: 979-8-88679-578-3

**Dedicated to**

*Dewey Albert Severs*

*1941–2020*

*Carolyn Saddie Severs*

*1940–2018*

**Sons**

*William Jay*

*Dewey Lee*

*Allen Wade*

# CONTENTS

*Preface* ............................................................. 1

CHAPTER 1
My Childhood ................................................. 5

CHAPTER 2
Moving to Illinois ........................................... 14

CHAPTER 3
Out on My Own .............................................. 26

CHAPTER 4
Moving West ................................................... 30

CHAPTER 5
Carolyn, My Love ........................................... 32

CHAPTER 6
Firefighter and Farmer ................................... 39

CHAPTER 7
Wisconsin Dairy Farm ................................... 51

CHAPTER 8
Heart Attack .................................................... 59

CHAPTER 9
Teamster .......................................................... 63

CHAPTER 10
Move to New Mexico ..................................... 69

CHAPTER 11
My Boys .......................................................... 78

CHAPTER 12
My Life, My Wife, My Lord . . . . . . . . . . . . . . . . . . . . . . . . 85

CHAPTER 13
Dewey's Sculptures . . . . . . . . . . . . . . . . . . . . . . . . . . . . . . . 93

CHAPTER 14
Dewey's Poems . . . . . . . . . . . . . . . . . . . . . . . . . . . . . . . . . . 131

*Acknowledgments* . . . . . . . . . . . . . . . . . . . . . . . . . . . . . . . 147

*References* . . . . . . . . . . . . . . . . . . . . . . . . . . . . . . . . . . . . . 149

# PREFACE

It was the fall of 2003 when I met Dewey Severs and his wife, Carolyn. Saturday, November 29—a typical fall weekend in Raleigh, North Carolina, with warm days and cool nights. Every year on Friday, Saturday, and Sunday of Thanksgiving weekend, the annual Christmas Carousel Holiday Gift Market arts and crafts show is held at the North Carolina State Fairgrounds in Raleigh, an event I always looked forward to attending to get a jump on Christmas gift buying. It's a large show of two or three hundred craftspeople selling their handmade creations.

    I went up and down every aisle looking for bargains, and as I rounded the last corner, my feet and back were aching from walking on the concrete floors. I hadn't purchased a thing. A few booths from the end, I noticed a portly gentleman standing in the aisle wearing blue jeans, a plaid shirt, red suspenders, cowboy boots, and a cowboy hat. He looked a little out of place with the other exhibitors. In his booth was a display of black metal objects of various shapes and sizes. That distinguished-looking cowboy was Dewey Severs.

Dewey acknowledged me with some small talk, but being tired, I ignored him and went about looking at his display of artwork. Dewey then directed his attention to two ladies who had walked up about the same time I had. I soon realized that Dewey had never met a stranger and commanded attention from whomever he met. As Dewey and I talked, I was captivated by the conversation. He quickly drew you into his world, and you became a child wanting to be transported into his life of adventure. Every one of his sculptures and poems had a story and represented a life experience.

Dewey's reason for being in Raleigh was not only to exhibit at the craft show but also to see his son and his son's family. In the booth with him were his wife, Carolyn; his middle son, Dewey Lee; his son's wife, Kelly; and their son and daughter, Zachary and Kayla. Dewey and Carolyn hadn't seen their son and his family for a couple years. Dewey Lee was a gunnery sergeant in the US Marines stationed at Camp Lejeune in North Carolina.

As you follow Dewey from a life of poverty to creative genius, through many professions and seven states over almost eighty years, you will be reminded of your own life journey. There is a little bit of Dewey in all of us. Dewey's relationship with God was very personal and something he relied on for most of his life. Dewey was a national treasure.

My life has been enriched from knowing Dewey and Carolyn, as I hope yours will be from reading this book.

—Tom L. Arnold

CHAPTER 1

# MY CHILDHOOD

My name is Dewey Albert Severs. I was born April 10, 1941, near Oxly, Missouri, in the Ozarks. Oxly is in southeastern Ripley County, located on Logan Creek along Missouri Route 142, approximately seven miles east of Doniphan, Missouri. Oxly is a small town with a population of eighty people, as of 2023. Doniphan is the county seat of Ripley County. During the Civil War, most residents of the area identified as Southerners and fought for the Confederacy. In 1864, Union troops entered Doniphan and burned most of the town, including the wooden courthouse. The population today is almost all white. In 1900, Doniphan was still considered a sundown town that prohibited African Americans from living there. Sundown towns were also known as sunset towns, gray towns, or sundowner towns, which meant they were all-white municipalities or neighborhoods that practiced racial segregation. The term came from posted signs saying that "colored people" had to leave town by sundown. The practice was not restricted to Southern states. Some towns still practice this.

We lived in a log cabin near the river, close to Doniphan. The cabin had cracks in the walls big enough to throw a tomcat through. We didn't have running water or electricity, and there were so many leaks in the roof that when it rained, my momma set out pans to catch the rainwater. For our necessities, we had an old outhouse that was a sanctuary for spiders and bats.

To make money, my daddy cut railroad ties with a crosscut saw, a sledge, and a wedge. We didn't have a mule at that time, so Daddy carried the ties on his shoulder to the local landing. There weren't many bridges over the creeks in those days, so you might have had to wait till the water went down to cross the creek.

Daddy was tough on us kids. One of the hardest whippings I ever got was because I was playing with a fruit jar full of his drinking water that was sitting under a tree to keep the sun off it. My brother and I got thirsty while playing and drank all the water in the fruit jar. When Daddy came looking for a drink and found the jar empty, we got the beating of our lives. My daddy was a hard worker, though. He worked so hard he could take his blue denim shirt and hang it on a chair until the sweat dried, and it would turn real white from the salt. You could lean it against a wall, and it would stand on its own.

When living in the Ozarks back in the '40s, we didn't have names on the roads or addresses on the houses the way people have today. The properties people lived on were named for the families that had lived there for years and years. They were named for families that had homesteaded the area. So, a place might be called the Armsby place, the Buttermilk place, the Jullian Ray place, or the Everheart place. You would mention those names, and everybody in the county would know who you were talking about and where you lived.

Life was hard in Oxly, Missouri. My grandma lived in town, and we lived just outside Oxly on Logan Creek. Most homes didn't have electricity or running water or any modern conveniences. They had dirt streets like some of those old Westerns you see on TV. There was one general store, and it was the first place to get electricity and had the only telephone in town. Logging was how most people made their living in the '40s. I remember some of those old log trucks didn't have any fuel pumps, and since the gas was gravity fed to the engine, they would have to back up the hill to keep the engine running.

I remember it was about 1945 when my uncle Oxford Timmons came out to our place riding a motorcycle. We had never seen one before. He was on leave from the military on his way to the war in Germany—or maybe he had already been over there. I don't remember. That same summer, a real dirigible flew over our house. We looked up in amazement, having never seen anything like that before. It wasn't long after that they quit flying.

During my early years, we lived in some pretty rough-looking houses, including a tar-paper shack. I remember the day my brother put all our knives, forks, spoons, and any other little trinkets he could find down a hole in the floor. When Daddy found out about it, he had to tear up all the floorboards to get all our treasures back. In that same house, my momma and daddy heard my brother crying one night. While he was in bed, a mouse had been chewing on his finger. Of course they scared it away, but my brother carried that scar for the rest of his life. Things were pretty backward then.

I was probably about three years old, maybe four, when Daddy was down in the field a'plowin'. My brother was kind of ornery. We had a box full of potatoes. They had potato buds on them here and there. Anyways, my brother asked me to smell them. I smelled them, and he jammed one of those little potatoes up my nose. Well, it got caught up there. He got a bobby pin and tried to get it out. Well, it jammed it in further, and about that time, Momma came in and saw what had happened. She tried and couldn't get it out. I had a potato stuck in my nose. Momma ran down to the field where Daddy was, and he came up with the team. The transmission was out of the truck, so Daddy spent all night fixing it so we could go to the doctor's office in Doniphan. The doctor went up my nose with a scalpel and cut the tater out. The next thing the doctor did—and you don't see this today—was pick me up and bust my butt royally in front of Momma and Daddy. Then Daddy said, "He didn't stick it in his nose." The doctor said, "But he was damn fool enough to smell it." So, for the rest of my life, people have reminded me of that story.

Both my grandpas spent time in prison for bootlegging. I guess bootlegging would be something like those marijuana farms they have today. So, that's how they made money until they got caught.

Along with my grandparents, parents, brother, and sister, we had a lot of cousins that lived in the Oxly area. I don't know if you have ever heard of double cousins. Because it was hard to get anywhere without a car or truck, you walked, or if you were lucky, you had a wagon and a horse to get you where you were going. You spent most of your time with family and friends who were often kin. I guess that's how I ended up with double cousins. You see, Momma and Daddy, they married a brother and sister. If you swap them around, double cousins are closer than an actual brother and sister. My aunt Edith was my daddy's sister, and my uncle Homer was my momma's brother. Edith and Homer were married to each other. And so, we had double cousins about the same age as us.

Daddy courted Momma on a mule, and the mule looked somewhat like a horse because its ears were burned off. He talked a lot about that. My brother, Benny, he was a year late going to school because the only way he could get to the schoolhouse was to walk on a train trestle that was pretty high off the ground. Momma and Daddy feared the train would come along while he was on the trestle, so they held him back for a year. Daddy finally got a team of horses. I can remember them, Prince and Charley. Prince was a sorrel, and Charley was black, so they didn't look anything alike. But they worked really well together. Daddy could work them with no lines, and he'd plow the garden with them. I can remember one time I was standing there crying because one of the horses had crapped in the garden, and Momma said, "Quit crying. It's only fertilizer." But I kept on crying because it looked like crap to me.

My grandma Severs, she walked down the sides of the roads in the hollers looking for pokeweed and wild asparagus to pick. And if she was near a stream, she'd find watercress and cook greens for us to eat. It was kind of like having your own vegetable garden. Daddy, he would go out at night and gig frogs. He would take a forked piece of iron and stab a frog with it, and we'd eat the legs. Or maybe he would find turtles and bring them home to eat. I can remember working in the fields when I was really small. We'd drag sacks down the rows and pick cotton in nearby fields. You'd have to watch out for black snakes in the cotton fields. When nobody was looking, we'd eat the wild dewberries at the ends of the rows and sometimes lie down and fall asleep in the sun.

I can remember Daddy's first mule. He wouldn't pull anything. Daddy got him at a kill sale. A kill sale is where you take worn-out animals to sell to the glue factory. Daddy named him Hitler. I guess he associated him with World War II. Hitler wouldn't work. Daddy took him out and hooked him to a skid of logs to pull. He wouldn't pull, so Daddy unhitched Hitler from the skid, tied him to a sapling, and began to beat him with a log chain. They'd put Daddy in jail if he did that today.

He tried again, but Hitler still wouldn't pull, so he took him back over to the same sapling and beat him severely. He hooked him up again, and he still wouldn't pull. Daddy beat him so bad that he began to bleed. Momma said, "You're going to kill him," and Daddy said, "He is going to the glue factory where I bought him, and I'll damn sure kill him myself if he doesn't work." Well, I guess Hitler got the message, because he worked for Daddy every day after that. He wouldn't work for anyone else, just Daddy.

Sometimes Daddy and Momma would take us kids to the grocery store. I reckon it was four or five miles from home. That was before we had transportation, so we'd walk all the way. Coming home, Daddy would carry a hundred pounds of potatoes on his shoulder and lead my brother. Momma would carry a sack of groceries and me.

I can remember the first time I saw a steam engine train close-up. Daddy had taken a train to Chicago to pick up Grandpa Severs, who had died. They brought his casket home on the train, and we were at the station when they arrived. I can remember when the train pulled up to the station and let off steam. It scared me something fierce. I remember the train, but I don't remember seeing Grandpa's casket.

Daddy was a so-so musician and played the fiddle. He played old-time music at broom dances. A broom dance is a dance where you are short one lady. So, they use a broom for that lady. As you're dancing, you pat a guy on the shoulder and give him the broom and take his lady. Whoever ends up with the broom when the music stops has to go to his table and sit with the broom. Daddy was very much into drinking and playing the fiddle. He played old-time stuff like "Chicken Reel," "Leather Britches," "Goodnight, Irene," and "Under the Double Eagle"—songs you have probably never heard of.

We all remember the sounds of our childhood. I can remember when we got our first team of horses and went to town or wherever, maybe to Grandma's. Some of the best sounds I've ever heard were a horse's hooves clopping on the hard-packed dirt and the horses crossing a wooden bridge, the chain traces rattling and the wagon squeaking as we went down the road. We were poor and didn't have much, but family was everything and every day was an adventure.

CHAPTER 2

# MOVING TO ILLINOIS

It was about 1946. Times were hard, and Daddy was only getting about seven cents for a railroad tie. He decided we would move to Southern Illinois. There was more money to be made there. So, we loaded up all our belongings in a Ford Model A. Since it was a single-seated coupe, Daddy took the trunk lid off to make more room. My brother and I rode underneath a canvas in the trunk, and Momma and Daddy and Sis rode in the front. A friend drove an old truck with what little we had and followed us to Illinois. What I guess was only a 250-mile drive seemed like we were crossing the entire United States. Somewhere along the way, we had a fire under the dash, and it burned up all the wiring. Daddy had to lie under the dash and rewire the whole car. The wiring in that car was so simple that it wasn't too hard for him to figure it out.

We ended up in Cutler, Illinois, an area that had just started strip mining. That's where I started to school in a one-room schoolhouse with only ten kids and a teacher. I guess I went there close to a year. My parents worried about us going to school because it was rumored there was a wild panther in the nearby woods. They found some tracks, so Daddy got a bunch of guys and some hounds, and they hunted it down. It was very unusual because it was a black panther. I can remember having a big forest fire there. I was crying and looking out the window, and it was so bright, the sky was lit. I thought, *Well, maybe that's what it looks like in all the big cities with all the city lights.*

Shortly after that, we moved again to just outside Sparta, Illinois. We rented a house from a man by the name of Charlie Hood. Charlie had a tractor, and he still farmed with a pair of hinnies. Now, if you don't know what a hinny is, I'll explain it. The father of a mule is a jackass, and the mother is a horse. A mule is sterile. But if you reverse the breeding and use a stud horse on a jennet—a female donkey—you don't get a mule, you get a hinny. They are not as smart or as good of workers as mules. That's why the old-timers didn't have much to do with them. Us kids kept Charlie and the hinnies well watered. We'd go to the hand pump and fill a fruit jar and carry it to him. He was an old man and enjoyed having us carry him water.

When we moved to the Charlie Hood place, we got us a dog. Daddy got us one of those spotted firehouse dogs, and he was pretty. I think they are called Dalmatians. Daddy got a job working construction and was gone a lot. On one of his extended trips, the dog got rabies. He was lunging at the front door, the back door, and all the windows. It seemed like the light from inside set him off. He was a big dog, and it seemed he could tear out the windows at any moment. He was foaming at the mouth, and all of us kids were scared to death. Momma lured him to the back door and sent for my brother, who was the oldest by two years. She had him sneak out of the house. I don't know how he did that without the dog getting him. He ran for a mile to Charlie Hood's place, and ole Charlie came with a shotgun and put the dog out of its misery. I guess it was a matter of maybe sacrificing my brother to save the rest of the family.

Shortly after that, we started to McClinton School near Sparta. We had thirteen students and the teacher. We walked three miles one way to school. About halfway, we would pass the house of Pauline Boone, a black lady. "You all come up and warm your feet," she would holler. She lived in a one-room shack. We'd walk up there, and she'd open the door, and we'd go in and stick our feet close to an old stove that burned corncobs to get warm. Then down the road we'd go. Her sister didn't live too far from us either. Her name was Clara Boone. We always wondered if they were related to Daniel Boone.

We didn't wear shoes unless we were going to school or maybe to town, so we only got a new pair of shoes once a year. Since you only had one pair, you sure took care of them. I can remember one year we got an early snow, and the little kids down the road, the Gardners, didn't have decent shoes. They had lost their daddy in a tractor accident. They were in such bad shape that our teacher tore up her petticoat and tied rags around their feet so they could make it home in the snow. They had to walk about two miles with those rags around their feet.

Sparta was segregated in those days. The black people, they had their own restaurant, which probably was the only restaurant in town for them. We had a movie theater for the blacks and one for the whites. The black people always seemed to get the worst of everything. They couldn't drink in our fountains, and their movies weren't up to par with ours. Their schools weren't near the schools we had. They even had their own cemetery. They couldn't be buried with the white people. I can remember a black preacher coming out of St. Louis, Missouri. He was preaching trash and all that. They ran him out of town. But the amazing part of that story was that the white people didn't do it, the black people did. They got tired of all the problems he was causing.

My daddy drank a lot. Today they'd say he had a sickness, but we just considered him a drunk. We'd sit in the car and wait for hours while he drank away what little money we had. We'd cover up in the car with blankets until one or two o'clock in the morning. It seemed like every weekend for as long as I can remember. I don't know what year it was, but we had a 1938 Dodge. It had one of those suicide doors, where the rear door opened forward. We had just gotten it and had it only two days when it stalled on the railroad tracks near Sparta. We couldn't push it off the tracks, and it was snowing and blowing. It was close to Christmas, and we had all our presents in it. We were headed for Grandma's for Christmas. Well, Daddy ran back to town to get my uncle. He knew he would be in the bar. Momma and us kids decided to walk on to Grandma's, which was about a mile. Well, we got about a quarter mile, and we heard the train coming. This was the first time I can remember praying. Momma prayed, and we all knelt down on the road, and we all prayed. You could see the light coming and hear the train blowing that whistle. Then all of a sudden, the lights on our car went out and there was a terrible crash and there were bits and pieces of our Christmas and our 1938 Dodge for miles down the track. The car wasn't even paid for. As I said, this was my first recollection of praying.

I remember one time Daddy came home from work and gathered my brother and me up and said, "Alright, boys, I want you to find all the slingshots, your cap guns, and your rubber band guns. Or anything that looks like or that you play with like a gun." He said, "You're big boys now." I think I was in the second grade. He said, "From this day on, you aren't going to play with a pretend gun anymore." And he gave us a .22 rifle. It was a single shot. Daddy believed we needed to learn how to shoot a single shot. I still have that gun today. The problem was when I shot the gun, I couldn't hit anything. It made Daddy so mad he beat on me, whipped and cursed me, and everything else because I couldn't shoot that gun. I guess it was the following year, when I became a third grader, that the eye doctor came to school and said I needed glasses. Daddy said, "No way. He's just a kid. There isn't any way a kid of mine needs glasses." Well, Momma didn't listen to Daddy and took me to the eye doctor and bought me a pair of glasses. She never thought much about it, but the next time I got that gun out to shoot, I hit everything I aimed at. I could outshoot everyone in the family, including Daddy. Daddy set little bitty rocks up on a railroad tie, and we'd shoot at them, sitting on the back steps. From that day on, I could outshoot my brother with a rifle or pistol. Daddy never mentioned the glasses again.

The road in front of our house had a steep bank at the end of a sharp curve. One evening, we heard squealing tires followed by a loud noise. When we got outside, we saw that a car had run off the road and slid into the side of that steep bank. The force of the sudden stop had thrown the driver into the windshield and busted the windshield out. He was unconscious when we got to the car. Daddy reached inside the car and shut the engine off and drug the man out of the car. Daddy took him into the house and put him on the kitchen floor. Momma began washing his face with a wet cloth. When he came around, he said, "What are those lights? What are those lights?" Daddy said, "What lights?" He said, "The lights. They are so bright." Well, Daddy had gotten us a white double-mantle kerosene lantern, and it was bright. Maybe the man thought he was seeing the hereafter and was dead. Anyways, we got him patched up and sent him on down the road.

As I mentioned, Daddy was a drunk and couldn't leave the bottle alone. When he drove into the driveway, us kids would run to the window and watch as Daddy got out of the car. When he got close enough to the house for us to see his eyes, we could tell if he was drunk or not. If he was drunk, we would run out the back door and hide in the woods until he fell asleep. I remember one evening when Daddy came home drunk and began yelling at Momma and us kids. He became so angry that he had all three of us kids lined up against the wall and Momma sitting in a chair with a shotgun pointed at her head. It was one of those 12 gauges, a long gun. He had shells lined up on the table, one for each kid, and said that after he killed Momma, he was going to kill each of us. After a while, he put the gun down and drank himself to sleep. Us kids cried ourselves to sleep, and when we woke up the next morning, Momma had wrapped the gun around a telephone pole, and that was the end of a family heirloom. That was the last time he ever threatened Momma. To this day, I can look a person in the eyes and tell if they have been drinking.

That summer, by my memory, my brother and I took our .22 rifle and went to the river where we got our drinking water. It was about a quarter mile from the house through the woods. Being kids, we started shooting anything that flew, jumped, or crawled. When we got done, we realized we had killed a bunch of frogs and polluted that old water hole where we got our drinking water. We didn't have a choice but to tell Daddy what we had done. Well, Daddy was mad. The next night when he came home from the tavern, he had a bucket, a rope, and a narrow, pointed trenching shovel. It was summer vacation, so he took us outside and drew a big circle on the ground and said, "You boys are going to dig a holding tank right here." We worked all summer to dig that hole. When it was deep enough, Daddy filled the sides and bottom with wet cement. He put a wooden top on it, and we had a place to store rainwater or water hauled from town. At least we didn't have to carry water anymore. The only problem was that mice had a way of getting into it. Because of that, my sister always refused to drink water from that tank.

My brother, Benny, and I cut all our firewood, and occasionally Momma and us kids would walk down the railroad tracks and pick up pieces of coal that had fallen off the railcars. It would give us extra fuel for our woodstove. With our single-shot rifle, my brother and I would kill 250 to 300 squirrels a year. It takes two or three squirrels to feed a family of five. We ate a lot of squirrels.

At a very young age, I started working at any odd job I could find in order to have some spending money. I remember one time clearing four acres of sassafras brush so a neighbor could plant corn there. I used the fifteen dollars I made to buy a 16-gauge shotgun. I still have that shotgun. I guess it was about 1950 when I saw my first TV. I think I was in the fourth grade. The antenna cost more than the TV. That same year, Charlie Hood's oldest boy was killed by lightning while bringing in a load of hay with a team of horses. We helped Charlie with the harvest that year, and Momma helped cook for everybody working in the fields.

The following year, we moved into town—into Sparta. We had our first indoor bathroom, and I can remember Grandma Timmons saying, "Things are going to hell! People are doing their business in the house and eating outside!" To her, everything was backward. It was the first inside toilet I had ever seen. I can remember it was a two-story house, and when you flushed the stool, you could hear the water running through the pipes. Us kids would run down into the cellar and listen and say, "Where did it go? Where did it go?" We couldn't figure where in the world the waste went. When you look at kids today with their computers and stuff, it shows we were pretty ignorant back then.

Momma worked in Sparta at the largest comic book factory in the world. And Daddy was a town cop.

I guess I was about fifteen years old when Otis Pressler and Jerry Bailey started hounding me about going to church. I was fifteen when I found the Lord. I can remember standing in the back of the church listening to the preacher man preaching hell and damnation. As I listened, the hair on the back of my neck would stand straight up, and cold chills would run up and down my neck. I listened, but I wasn't going to walk down to the front of the church and be saved. I can remember this boy in school who drank beer and smoked cigarettes, and he probably was worse than me. So, I asked the Lord, "If you are for real, why don't you have this boy come to church and walk down there and be saved?" I didn't give that boy a second thought, and I never invited him to church. I still don't believe it, but the next week when I went to church, there he was, and he walked to the front and was saved. But you know what? I just thought it was a coincidence, and it was a long time later before I was saved and found the Lord. It was about the same time, due to disagreements with my daddy, that I left home.

CHAPTER 3

# OUT ON MY OWN

As I mentioned earlier, Daddy and I were having a lot of disagreements about me wanting to go to church. As a result, I decided to leave home. Daddy, he didn't agree. He didn't think I was old enough to know anything about being saved or walking down the aisle, joining the church, and being baptized. We had some real differences of opinion that created serious problems. I remember I had been out squirrel hunting and had left my muddy boots sitting on a newspaper in the kitchen. Daddy had been drinking when I came home from work about ten o'clock at night. I hadn't eaten anything, and being a school kid, I was starved to death. Daddy told me to clean up my muddy boots, and I said, "I will as soon as I get done eating." Well, he didn't care for that comment, so we had a big knock-down, drag-out argument. About that time,

I was driving a beat-up 1946 Ford. I put everything I owned in the car and told Daddy I was going to leave. He said I would come crawling back. I said I'd starve to death first, and I almost did.

I lived the first week on a half gallon of milk and a box of cereal. The night I left home, I went to my uncle's, and he turned me away. He said he didn't want to cause any problems with Daddy. I think he was afraid of him. I left and went to my other uncle's, and he said I could stay the night. I told him I would leave the next day before Daddy found out and caused my uncle trouble. The next day, I found two old ladies that had a room for rent. I found out later they were a mother and daughter. They seemed somewhat suspicious of me being so young and all. They put a refrigerator upstairs near my bedroom and a hot plate in my room to cook on. I got my drinking water from the bathroom down the hall. I lived the balance of my high school years with those two old ladies. The daughter was in her sixties, and her mother was ninety plus. I had a separate entrance in the back of the house to come and go. A friend of mine, Bill Keys, was concerned about what I was going to do for entertainment, so he took parts from two or three old radios and put them together. He made a wooden front for it, and I used that radio for a long time. After I graduated,

I was tired of looking at it, so I threw it away. The young man who made my radio went on to college and became some kind of electrical engineer. He must have known what he was doing.

It took every dime I had to live, so I never went to any school functions, like ball games or proms. I was too busy trying to make a living. I worked at the Kroger grocery store and cut brush on weekends for a dentist. And my brother, he worked in a filling station, and the two of us, when needed, hand dug graves for this old fella. We did that until he died, and then we dug his grave. I got Cs and Ds in school and just slid by. I went to the assistant principal's office and asked him if I could miss last period study hall so I could get in an extra hour's work each day. I told him I needed money really bad or I was going to have to leave school and go to the service. He allowed me to do that, and I could make an extra five dollars a week. That extra money was the difference between eating and going to the service. The only recreation I had was going to church on Sunday. When possible, I also went to church on Saturday, Wednesday, and Thursday nights. Everyone called me the Kroger kid because I worked there for four years. Everybody in the county shopped there.

When it came time for graduation, I didn't have enough money to rent a gown or go on the senior trip. Everyone said, "What are you going to do?" and I said they could just mail my diploma to me. On the last day of school, a lady by the name of Mrs. Bailey, Jerry's momma, gave an envelope to my best friend, Jerry, who gave it to me. There was enough money in the envelope for me to rent my gown and go on the senior trip. I broke my neck getting down to the school office so I could be part of it. By the time I graduated, I had become an A and B student. I did this by paying attention to what was going on in class. The year 1959 had come, and I had graduated.

## CHAPTER 4

# MOVING WEST

It was 1959, and I was out of school. After graduation, the Kroger store that I had been working at for four years offered me a job as produce manager. Wow! I couldn't believe it! Just out of high school, and I was a manager. I was very surprised when one night my daddy showed up at my door. I hadn't seen him for a long time. He said the family was moving to Colorado, and he would like me to go with them. He said my future lay in the west. I was surprised he asked me, but the thought of being away from family caused me to say yes. So, the whole family loaded up and went to Colorado.

When we got to Denver, me being a small-town country boy and all, I was downright lost. Before we moved, I had sold my car to have enough money for the trip and to start a new life when we arrived in Colorado. Not having a car meant I had to walk or take a city bus. We were living in a house on Broadway and Colfax in Denver. I had to take a bus all the way to the Aurora suburbs. I walked all the way from Fifteenth Street to Thirty-Ninth Street to catch the bus, a round trip of about twelve miles. I had never seen water sprinklers before, and I had to step off the sidewalk and walk in the street to keep from getting wet. When I got to a possible job location, I interviewed with the boss, and he told me to come back the next day for another interview. So, I walked all the way back to Colfax and caught the bus to Broadway. The next morning, I repeated the process and took the bus to Kearney and walked from Fifteenth to Fortieth. After three days of going back for interviews, I said to the boss, "Hey, is there a better way to get here?" He started laughing and said, "There is a bus stop a half block from here. You have to change buses in order to get where you're going, but you only have to walk a half block." Before I left, he said, "Come in here." He took me to his boss and said, "Mr. Polantis, I've got a young man here who wants a job." They hired me on the spot for a job at the McKesson & Robbins drug warehouse.

CHAPTER 5

# CAROLYN, MY LOVE

About a year after I moved to Denver, I met the lady that would become my wife. She was a good-looking young gal, and she had a horse boarded at Aurora Stables. I guess she took a liking to my big brown eyes, and we kind of fell in love. I spent most of my time hanging around the stables courting Carolyn. When I wasn't with Carolyn, I was working as a laborer 160 feet down in the ground building the Titan missile silos. These were the big missiles with nuclear warheads we were going to send to Russia if we had to. We were building them way out east of Aurora. I finally met Carolyn's folks, and we celebrated our first Christmas together. It was the first Christmas I had celebrated in about four years, and all I could do was sit there and blubber like a baby because they were so nice to me. It wasn't long before we loved each other so much we got married, in 1962. We were married for fifty-six wonderful years.

In the Bible, there is a scripture that says a man and a woman are not supposed to be unevenly yoked. You see, this is some pretty serious stuff. I was a Baptist boy, and Carolyn was a Catholic girl. Even though we believed in the same Lord, we still had a lot of differences. As a matter of fact, overseas they had fought wars between the Protestants and Catholics to the point of killing each other. Carolyn and I had considerable differences. To make peace, I put my Baptist religion on a shelf and took lessons on marriage vows and agreed my children would be raised Catholic. And we were married in the Catholic church. Being a Baptist, even though I studied Carolyn's religion and all that, I didn't join the Catholic church because I didn't believe that way. But they allowed us to get married so she wouldn't be excommunicated. We weren't married at the altar. We could only be married halfway up the aisle because she was marrying a non-Catholic.

As I sit here thinking about deer and elk hunting, I think about the very first time I went deer hunting. It was with Carolyn's daddy the year before we married. He took me to the Colorado Rockies. This was my chance to make a good impression with her daddy. They had a relative named Bill. He was probably in his mideighties. Bill was a heavy smoker, and nobody would take him hunting because he smoked. They were afraid because of his age and his smoking, he might die. But we figured if he was going to die, he might as well die doing something he liked. So, we took him deer hunting. Ole Bill quit smoking six weeks before we went so his wind would be good enough to ride a horse. We each had a horse to ride. Once, we stopped to eat, and they were sitting on some logs reminiscing about old times, which I wasn't interested in. I was more excited about it being my first time hunting deer, so I moved some distance away from them. I was sitting there eating my sandwich, looking at the beautiful country, when I saw the biggest deer I had ever seen in my life. I slowly took out my rifle, took aim, and shot the deer. I hollered and hollered, "I got him, I got him, I got him!" Every time I hollered, I ejected a shell from my gun. I had me a case of buck fever. When I turned around, there was Bill and Carolyn's daddy standing there laughing and laughing 'cause Dewey was ejecting shells instead of loading more into the chamber. It was my first deer hunt. There weren't many deer to hunt where I grew up. All we hunted were pheasants, quail, raccoons, groundhogs, and opossums. Nothing big like deer. It turned out to be only a two-point buck, but to me it was the biggest thing I had ever shot. We loaded it on a horse and took it back to the cabin, where Carolyn and my future mother-in-law were waiting. They told me that while I was gone, they saw a rabbit sitting on my bed. The cabin was pretty sparse, so anything could get in. At least it wasn't a grizzly bear.

  We were staying near Breckenridge, Colorado, which today is a major ski resort. It was near where ole Bill lived, which back then was just a wide spot in the road. Now the hard part began. I had to skin that deer outside in the dark with the help of a kerosene lamp. It was very cold, and I couldn't wait to get done and get in that warm sleeping bag. When I crawled in the bag, the first thing I found was a bunch of little bitty pellets. I had my long johns on because it was colder than billy hell. I soon realized that the rabbit they had seen sitting on my bed had left its calling card with a lot of rabbit crap. I jumped out of bed hollering, "That rabbit crapped in my bed!" They were laughing and laughing. I got a flashlight out and took another look. They had set me up…The joke was on me. My bed was full of raisins.

In 1964, we had our first child. His name was William Jay Severs, born August 31. He was named after his grandpa Spangler. I was so proud I think I bought cigars for everybody in Denver. This was about the time President Kennedy got shot. I remember everybody in the country was crying, and things were in big turmoil.

I remember just prior to Carolyn and I getting married, we went to my first rodeo. I was sitting in the grandstand watching her cousin, Leroy Coombs, in the bull-riding competition. He was about the same age as me. He was riding on one of those big Brahman bulls. I turned to Carolyn and said, "Someday I'm going to do that." She laughed, and it hurt my feelings. She said, "You really have to be strong to do that. You've got to know how to ride and really know what you're doing to ride on one of those bulls." Well, the second rodeo I was ever at, I was sitting on one of those bulls. I borrowed her cousin Leroy's gear, and he taught me how to do it. I hung on for dear life. I almost lasted the required amount of time before being thrown off. Not bad for a first ride. I did this until William Jay was born and decided that wasn't the best thing to be doing with a young boy to raise. So, my last ride was on a wild untamed bucking bronc in a rodeo at the Flying W Ranch in Colorado Springs. I can remember I got on the bronc, and I had a brand-new set of dentures. Carolyn was sitting in the grandstand, chewing on her fingernails as she always did when I rode. Anyways, the bronc cut up real bad in the loading shoot. I had accidentally spurred him in the side in the chute, and he was really turning on. He went up in the air, and I felt like I was sitting in a recliner, and when he came down, I hit the ground. All I could hear was my wife hollering in the grandstand, "You still got your teeth? You still got your teeth?" The crowd just roared with laughter. Because of the bad start, the judges wanted to know if I wanted a re-ride, and I said, "No, I am all done with this rodeo stuff."

Sometime around 1964, I got a job as a home delivery milkman. I worked for the company that invented the plastic bottle that you have today. The bottle started as a coin-sized plastic object, and they put it in a machine and blew hot air into it. It would emerge as a bottle and was instantly filled with milk. Never touched by human hands. No more dirty bottles.

In 1965, the Denver area had a major flood. The South Platte River flooded on June 16, 1965, and it was one of the worst natural disasters in Denver's history. It claimed a total of twenty-four lives. Fourteen inches of rain fell in four hours. Creeks overflowed, roads became rivers, and fields became lakes, all in a matter of minutes. They flew rescue helicopters for miles, picking people up off the tops of their homes. It seemed like there was no way out of Denver except by air. You couldn't drive far since many of the bridges were washed out. There were even chunks of asphalt going down the river with cars sitting on them.

It was about 1967 that I started breaking horses to harness. I did this as a hobby in my off time. I got my first team of horses named Ben and Babe. This was the beginning of a career that would be the foundation of what I did for much of my life. More about that later.

## CHAPTER 6

# FIREFIGHTER AND FARMER

It was 1968, and I was trying to get a job with the Boulder, Colorado, fire department. Being undersized and weighing only 135 pounds, I was eating bananas, drinking chocolate malts, and doing everything I could do to put on weight. When they finally hired me, I was the smallest fireman they had ever hired. I thought I had the world by the rear. I was a professional firefighter. The same week I hired on as a firefighter, they had 130-mile-an-hour winds coming down off the Flatirons. The wind broke the wind gauge at the fire station. It was like a hurricane without the water. It blew houses into the middle of the street. Downed power lines started fires everywhere. Seemed like half the city was on fire. We had fire engines coming from everywhere to help us. We had one firefighter blown off an engine and killed. We suspected that debris from a construction site knocked him off the engine. He was a volunteer. Sheets of plywood were blown off the sides of houses and piled up like a deck of cards. Squad trucks were driving sixty miles an hour trying to catch the flames of tall grass fires. At the airport, airplanes were ripped out of their tie-downs and torn all to pieces. A terrible night for my first week on the job.

Anyways, here I was wondering, What am I doing? I can remember being on one of our runs. In those days, we went out on bomb scares. We weren't very smart. What would we have done if we'd gone in and found a bomb? I can remember one time a bomb was supposed to go off at noon at the library on campus. We were in the library looking behind every book, so at 11:59 a.m., I said to the lieutenant, "Hey, don't you think maybe we ought to be getting out of this building?" He said, "Well, we still have a minute to go." I said, "Yeah, but what if the bomber's watch isn't exactly the same as ours?" So, we left the building, but the bomb didn't go off. In the future, we let the police go in looking for a bomb while we stood back and waited to pick up what was left.

Firefighters are all alike everywhere. During 9/11, we saw the great tragedy when the buildings came crashing down. Whether in small or big cities, we all live the same kind of stuff. I can remember one time when we were on top of a burning barn. Me, Trachler, and Deleplane. We were on the roof, and the rafters broke. I went through into the fire, fell maybe seven or eight feet. Deleplane lay down and reached for me with his hands and got me by the forearms, while Trachler held the fog nozzle on us. He throwed me over his shoulders, and we got off the roof together. That teamwork and dedication for each other saved my life. We did a lot of horseplay, but when the bell rang, it was all serious stuff. Every man would put his life on the line for his crewmates. We worked four days out of every ten—nine or ten days a month, depending on the month. But these were actually fifty-six-hour weeks 'cause you counted the night hours you were sleepin'. 'Course it was like sleepin' in a foxhole. You didn't sleep sound. I slept with my socks on so I could jump up and run and get on the fire engine real quick. Our performance was based on how quick we could do that. In the middle of the night when we were all asleep, we were upstairs, and the fire alarm would ring. The door would roll up, and we would hit the middle of the street in fifteen seconds. That's fully clothed and on our way out. People have a hard time believing that. That is compared to a bull ride, which is eight seconds. So, you can accomplish quite a bit if you are geared for it. I was at the department for about six years with the best bunch of guys that you would ever want to work with. We were like blood brothers 'cause we went through some pretty hairy situations together. We trusted in each other.

In my spare time, my wife and I dairy farmed. Carolyn and I bought a brand-new house at the same time our third and final son, Allen Wade, was born. My mother-in-law, Eunice Spangler, was very disgusted because she had all grandsons and no granddaughters. Allen Wade was a redhead. We had one of them crop up in every generation. My grandpa was redheaded, my brother was a redhead, and his son and my son were redheaded. After three boys, Carolyn and I figured out what was causing all that and went in and had me fixed so we could stop that nonsense. We never did have any little girls.

While I was at the fire department, we decided we wanted to farm part time. So, I sold our new house, and we took the money and turned it into tractors and farm machinery. Not new machinery but some really old stuff. Carolyn and I moved to the 160-acre Costlett farm near Lyons, Colorado. We started farming at the same time Colorado had a gasoline shortage. You could only buy a dollar's worth at a time. A farmer's gas allotment was prorated based on what he had purchased the previous year. Since we didn't have any previous purchases, we didn't have gas to farm. The only option was to do most of the farming with horses. I plowed, planted, mowed, and worked as many as four head of horses and put my spare time in at the dairy on the Costlett farm.

The first year, we had a surplus of grain and no place to store it, so we made what became a big mistake. We bought some dairy cows to milk. Carolyn milked cows while I worked at the fire department. I'd plow the fields on my time off, sometimes at night. Along with doing the milking, Carolyn would irrigate the fields. She'd walk the entire 160 acres while dragging the boys along by the hand. Sometimes it would be midnight or maybe one o'clock in the morning when she changed the irrigation water from one field to another. These ladies today, they don't know what it's like to take care of the little ones and put in a day's work. My wife worked hard.

It was 1970, and we had just bought a brand spanking new Volkswagen Bug. I really don't know why, but we just had a new baby calf. To move the calf, we let them seats down, and it made into a trunk space in the back end. We put the calf back there on a little bit of straw, along with our three boys, and drove to Aurora to show Grandpa Spangler the new calf. It was in the wintertime, and we were gone most of the afternoon. We came back that night since I had to be at the fire department the next day. The windows were all fogged up, and the boys were asleep in the back with the calf. I passed a car in a no-passing zone and got pulled over by a cop. Anyways, those Volkswagens had a high back behind the front seats. The cop was filling out the ticket for passing too late, and he took his flashlight and shined it in the back of the car. When he looked in the window, the calf became startled and mooed. It just scared the poop out of that cop. He shined his light in the back of the car, turned around and walked back to his car, got in, and drove off. He never finished giving us the ticket or anything. So, we figured he must have done something in his pants. He had to hurry and get back to the station. I reckon that cop probably thought that was the ugliest kid he had ever seen. Just one of the stupid things we did. A calf in a Bug.

Well, I have an even better story with that Volkswagen Bug. I had a grain drill with two horses, Tom and Jerry, hooked to it. I'd been in the field planting alfalfa for hay. I had about forty-five pounds of expensive seed left, and it was looking like rain. Sometime late in the day, the horses' mouths started to get a little sore in the corners, so I loosened up the bits a little bit, one notch. It was a steel wheel grain drill about ten feet wide. It was actually a tractor drill, but I had it fixed up for the horses. Before it rained, I decided to head for home, so I turned onto the road and followed Carolyn and the three boys in the Volkswagen down the road. We were about four miles from home. Well, Tom and Jerry were new and not very trustworthy. We got them from a ranch in Nebraska, and the cowboys who broke them just let them run. Anyways, when I turned out onto the road, the drill wheels hit something and made a loud noise, and them horses took off running. I was hanging on for dear life. There was a deep ditch and barbed wire fences on each side of the road. I knew if I got into a barbed wire fence, I would be in trouble. So, I just put my feet against the doubletree and lay back, holding on to them lines, hollering, "Whoa," until "whoa" wasn't doing any good. I was just trying to keep them in the middle of the road. They were frothing at the mouth and not slowing down. Finally, I screamed at Carolyn to get the car out front and use it as a wall to slow them down. I couldn't hold them much longer; my arms were wearing out. We had gone a mile or two before she drove around me. She caught them. She said she was doing thirty miles an hour. That's fast for two 1,600-pound horses. When she got in front of them, I hollered for her to start slowing down. All I could see was all three of my boys' eyeballs looking out the back window of that Volkswagen Bug. Three little pumpkin heads looking out. We were so close that the horses were ramming the tongue of the yoke into the trunk of that car. Bangin' it, putting a big ole dent in the back end. If she had stopped, those horses would have gone right over the top of the car. And there were those little boys looking out the back window. It worked; we finally got them stopped. We tied them to a telephone pole and went back home and got the trailer and loaded up the horses. One more of my famous runaway wrecks. After that, we carted off ole Tom and Jerry and got a big team of mules. Puss and Boots were their names.

We got contracted by some film production outfit and went near Colorado Springs to film a TV commercial for Folgers Coffee. That actor, Noah Beery Jr., he played James Garner's father, Joseph "Rocky" Rockford, in the television series *The Rockford Files*. I remember Noah; he always smoked a cigar. We had this team of horses pulling this hayrack that was eighteen foot long and nine foot wide, and we were coming up to a campfire to get a cup of coffee. Noah was driving them. Well, he was pretty handy, but I stood on the back of the rack out of sight of the camera. In case there was a problem and they had to reshoot the scene, I'd have to line up the rack and start all over. The first four hours, we must have reshot the thing fifty times. I had to drive around the prairie dog hills and get it lined up so Noah could do his thing. About noon, they decided it was time to eat. So, Noah said, "Come on, Dewey, let's go eat." And boy, they put on a real cook spread at those commercial shoots. Noah, he threw his cigar away, and we went and ate.

He was telling me about working with John Wayne and other great actors. When we got done eating, he reached into his pocket and didn't have any more cigars. Here was this great big wealthy movie star crawling around on the ground looking for a cigar butt. We couldn't believe it. But he found a little ole cigar butt, dusted it off, put it in his mouth, and lit it up again. He was quite a guy. Just like he was on TV, very much an everyday person.

Another time, this outfit came out to film a commercial on our thirteen acres of dry land oats that we were about to combine. My combine had a hole in it that I couldn't get plugged up, so we'd take one trip around the field and stop at the irrigation ditch to put more water in it. It was taking forever to get that field combined. They wanted me to stop, and I said, "What about my oats?" They said if we finished the filming, they would pay me for whatever my oat crop was worth. They paid me $400 for eight hours of filming. More than what my entire oat crop was worth. A good deal for Dewey.

It was about 1972, and I still worked at the fire department. A twenty-four-hour shift on, twenty-four hours off. Life was good. We still made time for square dancing and stuff like that for entertainment. Down the road about five miles, a farm came up for sale. It had an eight-stall milking parlor. We didn't know where we were going to get the money, but with the Lord's help, we were able to raise enough money to buy the farm. I can remember we were moving everything from one place to the other. We left the boys playing on the swing set at the old place five miles down the road while we were putting things away at the new home. We both looked at each other, and Carolyn said, "Oh my God, we forgot the boys!" Well, we went driving back to get them. As we got close to the house, here they came. They were about a quarter mile down the road, and they were snotty at the nose and crying, my oldest boy leading the way. They thought we had moved and left them behind.

It was 1976, the year of the Big Thompson Canyon flood. It was one of the worst natural disasters to ever strike Colorado, when a twenty-foot wall of water rushed through the canyon, claiming the lives of 144 people, 5 of whom were never found. The Big Thompson River is a tributary of the South Platte River, approximately seventy-eight miles long. It was the evening of July 31, 1976. Twelve inches of rain fell in less than four hours, more than three-quarters of the average annual rainfall for the area. It was around nine at night when a wall of water raced down the canyon at thirteen miles per hour, destroying 400 cars, 418 houses, and 52 businesses and taking out most of US Route 34. By daylight, there were hundreds of cabins, barns, cars, trucks, campers, and trailers in the river. Of those caught by the flood, many escaped by climbing the steep canyon walls. A temporary morgue was established in Loveland as helicopters and horseback teams were ferrying bodies out of the canyon. The town's sewer pipes ruptured, sending raw sewage down the river along with everything else. Over 800 people were rescued, most with one injury or another to their bodies—a lot of hurt arms, a lot of cuts and bruises, that sort of thing.

## CHAPTER 7

# WISCONSIN DAIRY FARM

It was 1978, and we decided to move to Wisconsin and buy a dairy farm. We loaded up all we could carry, including Grandpa and Grandma, and headed east. We felt like pioneers. Kind of reversed—we had gone west, and now we were heading back east. When Carolyn and I went to Wisconsin and found a dairy farm to buy, we made another mistake. When we first went there, it was summer. We were not familiar with the area or the climate.

The next time we returned, it was our move to the area, and it was wintertime. Lo and behold, we realized that summer was August 14, and the rest of the year was winter. It was around Thanksgiving when we arrived, and there was four feet of snow on the level and fourteen-foot drifts. We moved twelve miles outside of Thorp, in north central Wisconsin. We bought a working dairy farm and moved our own cows. Because of all the snow and freezing temperature, the cows remained in the barn, tied in their stalls. We cleaned the manure from the stalls by hand with a shovel. The tractor that pulled the manure spreader was frozen up most of the time, so we used a horse-drawn spreader to haul the manure to the field. It was a little 160-acre farm, average for those days, in the middle of Wisconsin. We saw the temperature drop to fifty-four degrees below zero, and we're not talking about the chill factor. The snow was so deep that without a pair of bear-paw snowshoes, you needed to roll or crawl to the barn. The snow was so powdery and dry you couldn't walk in it. We'd have to take a crowbar to break the door loose from being frozen shut. Because of the body heat of the cows, it was warmer in the barn than in the house. That was winter in Wisconsin. Didn't take long before us menfolk learned that when you went outside, you carried a hammer in your back pocket. If you had been there, you would know that if you stopped to pee, you would have to break yourself loose with the hammer. If anyone died, the ground was frozen so solid that you couldn't bury them. You just stood them on the back porch and let them freeze solid until spring came and you could dig a grave.

The long winter gave me a lot of time to reflect on when I was a teenager and some of the spiritual things that happened to me. Like all kids at some time during their life, I was burdened, and I didn't know if the Lord was really there or not. I kept praying to the Lord because I didn't know if he was real, and I needed some kind of proof. Being from Missouri, the Show-Me State, I can remember being about fourteen or fifteen years old, lying in bed, praying to the Lord. I prayed, "Lord, if you're really there, take an arm or leg, take my eyesight, but prove to me one way or another that you exist." I fidgeted and squirmed from nervousness in bed and kept praying, but he never took an arm or leg, and I still could see, so I said, "Well, Lord, do something. If you're really there, make the bed fall down instantly!" We lived in a two-story house, and you know the bed fell down! I was so scared! It was unbelievable. The slats had fallen out from under my mattress, and the mattress landed on the floor. Momma and Daddy and my brother and sister came running upstairs. I was too scared to tell them that I had been praying and what had happened. But I guess the Lord answered my prayer. I still wasn't convinced the Lord existed. I thought these happenings might just be coincidences.

One day, I was sitting in the church in the back row. I was one of those back-row Baptists. The preacher was asking anyone who wanted to be saved to come down to the front of the church and accept the Lord as your savior, but I just wasn't going to do that. I stood in the back row, getting real nervous, gripping the back of the seat. To this day, I don't know what happened, but the next thing I knew, I was in the middle of the aisle walking toward the front. By this time, I was too embarrassed to turn around and go back. When I got to the front, the preacher man led me to the Lord. I was about fifteen years old, and my prayers had been answered. Sometimes I put the Lord on the shelf until things got dark outside. When I was sick or financially strapped and things like that, I would go to the Lord and beg and plead for him to bail me out. Sometimes he would, sometimes he wouldn't.

During the time we were in the dairy business in Wisconsin, Ronald Reagan was our president. During that time, there was a surplus of milk, so the government lifted the price controls. We borrowed money, and our dairy farm was highly financed. Some of us went in deep, some of us didn't. We were involved in a recession. A recession is when your neighbor can't get a job and he's havin' problems. A depression is when it happens to you. The result of government policy changes and the recession caused a lot of farmers to go belly-up. Land values declined, and operating loans weren't available. It took some time to realize what had happened. We couldn't borrow money to buy a cow. We couldn't borrow money to operate our dairy business because there was a surplus of milk. We had the place financed where they would take the payment right out of our milk check. When price controls were lifted, we lost one-third of our income.

You can live on beans, but you really need some meat. Well, now if you were to go down to the barn and butcher one of your cows, the bank would come out and count your cows. You better have every one of them. So, we had all kinds of meat standing in the barn. We had to do something. We learned how to tie or tape a flashlight to a .30–30 and step out in the cornfield and turn on the flashlight and shoot a deer. It was a $1,800 fine for poaching, but we were hungry. I can remember it was winter and twenty to twenty-five below zero. Me and the neighbor man and my boys, we went deer hunting down by the river. Well, there we were, standin' on the bank, and I shot this deer on the other side of the river. It was twenty-five below. So, I decided I'd wade the river and get the meat. So, we walked back up the river to where the water wasn't as deep. It wasn't frozen there. Well, I went in. I had on wool pants and a shirt and boots.

Oh, it was cold. You could hear me screamin' and hollerin' for miles. I got across the river. I took off all my clothes and wrung them out, emptied my boots, and put everything back on. Then I ran down and got the deer. Well, now I had to go back in the river again. Oh, it was terrible. So, I went back in the river in waist-deep water with the deer over my shoulder, trying not to fall. I didn't want to get my upper body wet. When I got across the river, my boys grabbed the deer, and my neighbor, Bob, being a big fella, throwed me over his shoulder. I was starting to go into shock. Bob took me a half mile to the truck and started it to warm me up. He drove me home and then went back for the boys and the deer. We did what we had to do to eat. We split the meat with the neighbor man.

In less than one year, three of my neighbors hung themselves from the rafters in their barns because they were losing their farms. These were farms that had been in their families for generations. Maybe you had enough money to fill your truck with gas, load your personal belongings in a U-Haul trailer, and head out for the Wisconsin border. On the way, you would stop and call the banker and say, "We can't take it anymore. The cows are in the barn, the hay is in the loft. You better find someone to milk them because we're hittin' the state line right now." There were many farms in the area you could take over by making the payment. It was the end of the dairy business for us in Wisconsin. I prayed to the Lord to find us a way out. He did. The way out was we would sell our livestock and machinery, pay off our debt load to the bank, and take any cash we had left to pay feed companies and other bills. We would give the farm back to the government because we couldn't sell it. Anyways, we managed to get all our stuff sold. Usually at 50 percent on the dollar. If you had a $1,600 cow, you were lucky to get $750. So, our assets just blew away.

We had very little left when we drove out of the driveway. We had a pickup and a camper. We bought the camper so we would have a place to sleep on the trip west. We also had Grandma with us; Grandpa had died in '82. Our caravan included Grandma pulling a U-Haul, Carolyn driving our car and pulling the camper, and me pulling a horse trailer with everything we had left in it. We all had handles for our CB radios. My wife was Milkmaid, I was Ruptured Duck, and Grandma was Gray Goose. So, we took off across the US for California. We had an aunt out there, so that's where we headed. It was quite an adventure. We stayed at fairgrounds and so forth along the way. When we stopped, we would tie the dogs and cats to the bumper. We ended up in Redding, California. I got a job at a large dairy farm. I became a foreman on a construction crew. They were building a methane plant to convert cow manure into electricity. Carolyn got a job in town as a bookkeeper. I had worked as a construction foreman for about a year when I landed a job with Dr. Dick Alley.

## CHAPTER 8

# HEART ATTACK

I was forty-six when I had my first heart attack. I nearly died. I lost use of one-third of my heart. I was interviewing for a job as a hitch driver with this lady in the mountains of Colorado. At that time, she had a drunk working for her. During the interview, I told her I didn't drink. I know she questioned my honesty because I was so sick, I was sweating and pale. I had been having chest pains all day long. She must have assumed I was in the bottle just like the last guy.

After the interview, the wife and I drove back to Denver. I told Carolyn I felt so bad I didn't want to drive all the way across Denver to the rooming house we were staying at. I said, "Let's just get a motel." Carolyn said, "Oh, honey, it's only just a few more blocks." I told her I couldn't make it, so we stopped and got a motel room. We went in, and she put me to bed. She said, "I'm going over to get our clothes and stuff so we can leave here in the morning." I lay there and lay there, and when Carolyn finally returned, I said, "You call the hospital and see how they are treating this flu." "Well," they said, "get him down here now." I would rather have taken a horse whipping than gotten out of bed and gone to the hospital.

When we got there, they put me on a heart monitor, shoved an IV in my arm, and put me in a bed in the emergency room. They also gave me oxygen. Before I fell off to sleep, I told Carolyn to go back to the motel and rest. Well, about midnight or so, my heart monitor started acting up. It was going crazy. I woke up and thought I was dying. Sure enough, my vision was narrowing in, and I was kind of pulling away. I kept praying, *Lord, spare me. I'm not ready to die, Lord. I'll be good. I'll walk with you if you just spare me.* Anyways, I kept wondering if there was a light at the end of the tunnel like they all talked about. And of course, I didn't know if it would be heaven's light or hell's fire that I was going to see. I was very much into prayer.

The nurse came running in with an IV in her hand. It was squirting in the air, and she hit me in a vein, and it was red hot throughout my body. About that time, she said, "You shouldn't be conscious." My heart was in a spasm. They hit me with a defibrillator as a last-ditch effort to bring me back. And it must have worked because I haven't told a fib since. The next thing I remember was waking up in the emergency room. The doctor said I had lost use of one-third of my heart and I was in terrible bad condition. They said I couldn't go back to work for at least a year. And sure enough, it was a year before I was able to do much. It put a hurt on us financially. But the Lord spared me, and I walked with him for six to eight months. As I felt better, I decided I could walk alone, so I put the Lord back on the shelf.

Then, about age fifty-one, it was boom—I had another massive heart attack. But as always, being from Missouri, the Show-Me State, it took three near-fatal heart attacks before I totally accepted the Lord. After each heart attack, I lay in a hospital bed preparing to die and begged the Lord to spare me. After each time he spared me, there was that little clock on the wall that was showing me how much time I had left. After my last heart attack, I had only 20 percent of my heart still pumping blood. About 50 percent of my heart muscle was gone. At fifty-one years of age, I had open-heart surgery. My insurance company found loopholes to deny payment and didn't pay any of the $80,000 bill. That was for eight days in the hospital. We wound up having to file bankruptcy and lost everything we had. This was about five years after we got out of the dairy business. So, what little we had managed to recoup after the loss of the dairy farm, we lost it all again. But on the bright side, the Lord had spared my life. After the loss of all material things in our life, I started to walk with the Lord and have been walking with him ever since.

## CHAPTER 9

# TEAMSTER

After we were in California for about a year, I landed a job with Dr. Alley. We were about twenty miles from the Oregon line. This was where I started my draft horse career driving six-, eight-, and ten-horse hitches. I worked for Dr. Alley for about five years. He was a heart doctor and eventually died from heart problems at age fifty-three. This would be, oh, somewhere around 1985. I was irrigating and making hay on two different ranches. I was takin' care of Dr. Alley's place, and his wife was married before, so she also had a place I was takin' care of. They had forty broodmares, not counting the colts we were raising. So, I was breakin' and trainin' and showin' and burnin' both ends of the candle. At Dr. Alley's, there was an old-fashioned hay barn that I redid. I put rings on the posts and installed a gate behind it where I could park a wagon. I could put six or eight head of horses tied to the swing poles, where I could harness them. When I got them all hooked up, they were standing there with the gate in front of them. The gate was spring loaded, so when I got ready to leave, I would unhook each of the horses, get up on the wagon, gather up the lines in my hand, and open up the gate. This whole process was accomplished by just me, and I was ready to drive on out of there. I could drive eight head of horses all by myself. We broke, trained, showed, and sold horses up through Idaho all the way to the Canadian line.

When I wasn't working for Dr. Alley, I was showing for other people. I can remember going down to Cambria, California, to meet with Ralph Covell. He had Clydesdale horses. His wife was in the hospital having a baby, and I was just brand new with him. They had paid for her to enter a driving competition class for ladies driving a team. They couldn't find a replacement for her, so they dressed me up in a dress and fixed me up with some boobs, put lipstick on me, and gave me a real fancy wig and white gloves. I drove that rig. As far as I know, I'm the only fella to ever drive in the woman's competition class. I got on that wagon and went around the ring, and the judge had no idea what was going on. As I went around the ring, the crowd would roar 'cause I would shake my hankie at them and wave. It was an awesome sight. If they looked close, the crowd could see my hairy leg stickin' out from under that dress. They found out that if you dared Dewey to do something, he would probably do it.

In my life, I've worked hundreds of horses and mules. During that time, I've had lots of runaways. When that happened, I learned to stay calm and cool when all hell's breakin' loose. When they are runnin', you keep your voice calm. If you start getting squeaky, the horses will start sayin', "Yeah, sure enough, we know something is wrong." But if you stay calm, the horses will think everything is okay.

At this time in my life, the extent of my drivin' is teaching people how to drive safely and get through the basics. Sometimes I feel like I have lots of experience just wasting away. Recently, I was surprised by a little neighbor girl of ours. She's about fourteen. She waters our plants when we're gone. She was rantin' and ravin' about a movie she saw. The movie was about a guy who drove a six-team hitch of horses all the way across the United States. And on the drive, he got married. And I said, "Really?" And she said, "Yeah, would you like to see the movie?" I said, "I know who he is." She said, "Oh yeah?" I said, "That's David Helmuth." She said, "How did you know that?" I said, "I used to work and show against David in the show ring. Matter of fact, if you look real close in the movie, you will see two of them horses, Spike and Cody. I used to drive them in my hitch in Indio, California." She said, "Really?" So, I showed her a bunch of pictures, and she couldn't believe it. Here was a fourteen-year-old girl in New Mexico, and the old man next door, he don't know nothing from nothing, and come to find out she was watchin' this movie about David Helmuth driving his six-team Belgian horse hitch from Maine to California. They traveled 3,600 miles, and it took sixteen months. David was an Amish fella from Iowa and did something everyone said was impossible. She was surprised this old man used to work with the same horses.

Years later, I was in Willard, New Mexico, with Lowell Clark when this fella came walking across the street and looked in the car and said, "Well, Dewey Severs, what are you doing here?" And I looked at him and said, "David Helmuth, you've gotten old, and you're fat." And of course, Lowell could see right away that we really did know each other. So, David said, "Dewey, why don't you go out of town with me? We've got the hitch out there. Two of those horses you used to work with. We drove them across the United States." We did, and it was Spike and Cody. Over the years, I worked with some of the best drivers in the country. What a small world it is. Well, as you can tell, I've lived everywhere and done a little bit of everything.

I worked with most all the different draft horse breeds, there being five main breeds of draft horses. Let's see, you have Clydesdale, Shire, Belgian, Percheron, and Suffolk. I only worked with one Suffolk in my life. Dr. Alley had one. Her name was Martha. She was the very best horse I ever worked. You could do literally anything with Martha. I've driven two as a regular team; three, four, and five abreast; and four, six, eight, and ten strung out. I was a pretty good teamster. I guess it is something born into you.

My youngest boy, Allen Wade, was up on the seat with me all the time, and he took care of the harness. He knew where everything was at, and I'd get up on the wagon and tell him, "Well, go down there and take the swing horse and raise the bit up in her mouth one notch, or do this or do that." He became a pretty good teamster. He also became a farrier and opened Severs Horseshoeing.

When we got to California, before working for Dr. Alley, I worked for a man in Newhall with his mules, drivin' ten-mule hitches for him. He had three ten-mule hitches, and we showed them in parades. He had a twenty-six-acre ranch in the middle of Newhall. There were skyscrapers all around us. He was offered millions of dollars for his place, and he'd say, "Well, where am I going to keep my mules?"

CHAPTER 10

# MOVE TO NEW MEXICO

We were living in Southern Illinois when I had my third heart attack. I was working as a farm manager. That's when we found out the insurance company wasn't going to pay for my medical bills. Just our luck. After we did our crying, we decided we had to move. We took our last $500 and bought an old 1957 one-ton Chevy truck. We patched up the rust holes with Bondo. I hitched it to an old horse trailer loaded with the few belongings we had left, and we limped all the way from Illinois to New Mexico. Two of our sons were there, and we wanted to be close to family. I was looking for a rock to crawl under so I could hide. I was ashamed of the bankruptcy. I couldn't talk about it without crying.

After we arrived in New Mexico, we rented a mountainside house from a lady who had gone to Arizona. We left most of our stuff in the horse trailer and took care of the house for a few months. While we were there, I slipped into deep depression. Nobody wanted me. I couldn't find a job. A complication from my heart surgery had left me temporarily without the use of my left arm. I could barely dress myself. I was fifty-one years old and felt useless. I looked out the kitchen window at the Sandia Mountains, glowing like embers in the New Mexico sunset. I could hear Carolyn in the living room tearing open and unpacking the moving boxes. She had me rest a spell, knowing how easily I got winded from my recent heart bypass surgery. Just gazing at the lush juniper and piñon trees on the mountain slopes made me feel old and tired.

    I got out of my chair and walked to an unopened box lying on its side in the corner. I turned it over with my right hand, as my left arm was almost useless from surgery complications. I picked up a box cutter and sliced through the packing tape. I was leaning against the wall, hoping Carolyn couldn't hear me trying to catch my breath. Inside the box were items from various jobs: wood planks, nails, and horseshoes. I was thinking I was as useless as this old junk. All my life, I had done hard physical labor. I was a fireman, farmer, milkman, construction worker, and carpenter. My favorite job was as a teamster. I had trained draft horses to show in competition around the country. Just four years earlier, I'd been able to drive a ten-mule team—then came three heart attacks. The huge medical bill drained our life savings. It still made my blood boil to think about the furniture I'd built, the pictures on the walls, and Carolyn's jewelry, taken away piece by piece and sold at auction. Now that we were here, I wanted to find a rock to crawl under to hide from the world of people who still contributed to society. I dragged the box of scrap to the garage and then went back inside to rest.

Within the week, Carolyn found a job as a bookkeeper to pay the bills. Watching her get ready for work one day, I slammed my coffee mug down with all my energy. "I can't stand this anymore," I shouted. She said to me, "For heaven's sake, Dewey, what is it?" "I'm just a burden on you," I said. "I've lost us everything, and now I'm good for nothing." She held my face with her hands and looked me straight in the eye. "Dewey, I've never known you to be a quitter. Don't start now." I began searching for work. Most people took one look at my arm and shook their heads. I finally managed to get a job as a carpenter. I couldn't work fast enough, so the boss let me go. I was too weak to do anything I was trained for, and I had never worked in an office.

At fifty-one, I had lost my health, my money, and my pride. What did I have left?

Carolyn kept encouraging me, but I got more and more depressed. I thought back to other hard times in my life. I had left home at age sixteen and began working seven days a week, but I still made time to go to church every Sunday. The Lord got me through all those tough months. After I married Carolyn and life smoothed out, I sort of put the Lord on a shelf. Now that times were rough again, I needed the Lord's guidance more than ever. When I tried to pray, all that seemed to come out was self-pity. *What's the point of living anymore, Lord?* I often wondered. I slept most of the time. Carolyn would come home from work and try to get me out of the house, sometimes just to walk across the field between our house and the mountains. "You just can't lie around the house all day, Dewey," she would say. "It's not like you." She never pushed me about working, but sometimes she forced me out of the house to take drives through the countryside. I could feel the tension between us. *Lord*, I prayed, *show me what to do.*

One spring afternoon, I awoke before Carolyn came home. Those of us who have been depressed know you want to sleep all the time. Because of that, a funny thing happened. I started having dreams.

I'd had dreams before, but I never remembered them being in color. These were in color and in great detail. I would wake up, go to the bathroom, come back to bed, and slip into the same dream. In my dreams, I would see little horseshoe sculptures. I felt like God was trying to show me something. I was striking a horseshoe with a pair of tongs, shaping it into something. I could feel the coolness of the tongs against my palm, hear the clash of metal on metal. The sensation of physical labor, even in a dream, was wonderful. One day, I awoke with an image of a cowboy and a mule sculpted out of a horseshoe. I sketched the image on a piece of paper and tucked it away in a drawer. Night after night, I dreamed of making sculptures by splitting and folding horseshoes.

One day after Carolyn went to work, instead of going back to bed, I pried open the rusty lid of my toolbox and found a blacksmith hammer. I went out to the garage, where an old anvil I had used in my teamster days stood behind some empty boxes. I dragged it to the center of the garage, my heart pounding from exertion. I grabbed a horseshoe from the box of scrap. I lifted the hammer in my right hand and swung at the horseshoe. The cold steel was hardly dented. I swung a few more times, accomplishing nothing more than giving myself a throbbing headache. *What made me think I could do this? Dewey, you're a fool.* The dreams kept coming. I'd wake up in the middle of the night and sketch the images I'd seen. One day, I dragged myself to the garage and stared at the dented horseshoe on the anvil. I thought, *It's so clear*, visualizing the cowboy I wanted to make. I took a deep breath and pounded the metal for about half an hour, resting often. The aches in my muscles actually felt good as unused parts of me were coming back to life. It had been months since I had felt this good. That evening, I told Carolyn about the dreams. I told her I felt like the Lord was guiding me. I told her, "I just feel like I have to make these things." She eagerly scrounged up more horseshoes from our moving boxes. Each day, I fought and worked with the metal, driven by images I had dreamed about.

After a few weeks, I finished a crude metal sculpture of a cowboy. I showed it to Carolyn. "This is wonderful," she said, hugging me. "I told you you'd find something to do. You should try to sell it." Sell it! Who would buy a mangled-up horseshoe from an old teamster? I didn't think of it as art, just something I did to get myself out of bed. I visited a local farrier to get more horseshoes. When I showed him my sculpture, he gave me a broken forge that I repaired. With it, I could heat metal so it was easier to shape. I was getting stronger every day, energized by the dreams and the work. After a few months, I had completed a dozen statues. I used scrap metal to fill in small details. Carolyn kept pushing me to sell them. We needed the money. "My friends at work love the one on my desk," she said. So, I finally gave in.

One Saturday morning, we packed the sculptures in an old dusty suitcase and drove to Albuquerque's Old Town. At the first store, I showed the sculptures to the store manager, and he said, "Did your grandkids make these?" Embarrassed, I shoved them back into the suitcase, and we left in a hurry. I felt like the local American Indians trying to sell their jewelry. I continued to show a single sculpture to any store employees at the craft stores we went into. We got the boot from store after store. It hurt my pride to walk down the sidewalk beside Carolyn, allowing her to lug around the heavy suitcase. "Last try," I whispered to Carolyn as we walked into Treasure House, a tiny shop jammed from floor to ceiling with novelty gifts and crafts. The man at the counter was the store owner. I showed him two of my creations. One was a cowboy sitting under a windmill, reading the deed to his land, the other a cowboy putting up a barbed wire fence. The owner picked them up and looked them over. "What are they made of?" he asked. "Some old horseshoes," I said. He eyed me sharply. "You make these?" "Yep," I said. My toes squirmed in my boots. "I'll take 'em," the owner replied. "Have any more?" Carolyn and I dug out the rest of the sculptures, and when we left the shop, the suitcase was empty and light enough for me to carry.

I went to work with a new purpose in life. Instead of shaking me awake in the evenings, Carolyn had to coax me to bed at night. I continued to sell my pieces to local shops and even got a booth at the New Mexico State Fair. In 1995, we sold enough sculptures for Carolyn to quit her job. The specialists at the New Mexico hospital helped me regain the use of my left arm. This allowed me to devote myself full time to my business. Carolyn ran the business side of things. I still get some of my best ideas from dreams.

Five or six years after selling my first sculpture, they are now found in several countries. I think about all the people who bought my early sculptures and encouraged me to make more. My early product was so bad that a year after I started making them, I used to go and look for them and buy them back and trade them out with new stuff. I would actually melt them down, they were so bad.

With people buying my work, it allowed us to have money to live on and for me to practice and go on and be more creative.

When my old life fell apart, I thought my best days were behind me. Now I know there was a new life waiting to take shape. God gave me the tools, the skills, and the vision. All I had to do was follow my dreams.

## CHAPTER 11

# MY BOYS

Besides marrying my wife, Carolyn, the greatest achievement in my life is my three sons: William Jay, born August 31, 1964; Dewey Lee, born January 24, 1968; and Allen Wade, born August 2, 1969. Between the three boys, they have six children, two each. Also, we have four great-grandchildren. My firstborn, William Jay, is a racehorse trainer. He lives in Oklahoma City and works at racetracks in Louisiana and other western states. He's got a boy named Colton Cade and a daughter named Casey Lane. And his wife is Carolyn S. Severs, same as my wife. My middle son, Dewey Lee, lives with his family in Texas. His wife is Kelly, and their son and daughter are Zachary Lee and Kayla Ann. He is retired from the military and works for Homeland Security. My youngest, Allen Wade, lives near us in New Mexico. His wife is Mandy, and they have two sons, Cody Ray and Clayton Wade. He is a farrier and teamster. None of them fell far from the tree.

I've got a lot of grandkids, and I have a hard time keeping up with their ages and names and stuff and all that. When my first boy, William Jay, was born, his grandpa cried, "I can't believe it. You named him after me, W. J." And then the second boy came along, and he couldn't believe it because my second boy was born on his birthday. Well, Grandpa had always said, "Well, ole Dewey would fall into a bucket of poop and come out smellin' like a rose." Sure enough, all them years later, my boy Dewey Lee's first boy, Zachary Lee, was born on my birthday. Now it's up to Zachary Lee to see if he can keep up the tradition.

My middle boy, Dewey Lee, went into the US Marines and was in some kind of intelligence operation. Because of that and him being up for a promotion, they were doing background checks on him and his family. They ran a background check that included his daddy and his granddaddy. Well, they called my son in, and they said, "Alright, young man, we want to know, what in the world is your daddy running from?" And he said, "What do you mean?" And they said, "Look at all these places he has lived." And boy, did he have a hard time trying to explain all that. But finally, they accepted it, and he got promoted. Dewey Lee was stationed at Marine Corps Base Camp Lejeune in Jacksonville, North Carolina, when Carolyn and I visited them in Raleigh and then was transferred to Virginia. He made master sergeant, as far as he could go without being a college person. So, I'm pretty proud of that young man. Because we lived all over, my sons suffered from that and had to prove themselves throughout life.

Back when Dewey Lee was promoted to gunnery sergeant, he called me and said, "Would you do me a favor, Daddy?" And I said, "What's that, son?" He said, "Would you come and pin my insignia on me? My badges on my lapel." And I said, "Well yeah, son, I recon I can. I pinned your diapers on, so I guess I can pin on your Marine Corps medals."

Two of my boys, Dewey Lee and Allen Wade, both served in the Marine Corps. I can't talk about it without crying. Lo and behold, the Gulf War came along. It took two of my boys to war. I told my wife, I said, "Honey, this is going to be one of those Vietnams. Prepare yourself; we may lose one of our boys." I got some amazing pictures of them meetin' on the battlefield the night before the battle actually started. They weren't in the same battalion. One was drivin' a vehicle, and one was in the trenches along the beach. As the one was drivin' a truck, he spotted his brother. How he did that I don't know, because their heads were buzzed and with their uniforms, they all looked the same. But they both came home from the war.

Dewey Lee and his wife, Kelly, had never learned much about church or anything. We took them to church. The preacher gave the invitation to be saved. Kelly said, "You know, I want some of that Jesus." And she got up and walked down front and accepted Jesus Christ as her savior. Then my wife got up and walked down to sit by Kelly, and she accepted Jesus Christ as her savior and was saved. My wife wanted to join my church. So lo and behold, we were no longer unevenly yoked. When the time was right, that was when he hooked us up evenly. Me being a Baptist and her being a Catholic, we were now the same.

I want to tell you about my middle boy, Dewey Lee. He was, oh, probably in the first grade. We'd been to a rodeo. My oldest boy was four years older than Dewey Lee. So, we had these young calves in the dairy barn and bottle-fed them and everything till they were up and pretty good sized. Anyways, my boys were into this rodeo stuff. I was sittin' in the house havin' my morning breakfast and coffee when I looked out the window and couldn't believe my eyes. Dewey Lee was on one of those calves, and they turned him loose, and he was drug all over the place. I jumped up and ran out and grabbed hold of him and, with my pocketknife, cut him loose. They feared he wouldn't be able to hang on and ride, so they tied him on with baling twine. Well, I got to tell you, they all got their britches warmed, and they were done with this rodeo stuff for a while. I told them, "You just don't tie a fella to a calf. You could get drug to death."

We were in Wisconsin on the dairy farm. Allen Wade, my youngest son, probably in the seventh or eighth grade, was being ornery when we were in the barn milking cows. In the milking parlor, we had a gutter used for the cow manure. It was about eighteen inches wide and eighteen inches deep and plumb full of cow urine and poop. Allen Wade was giving us a lot of trouble, and it was about thirty below outside. When we finished milking, my other boy and I grabbed him and hoisted him up by his belt and hung him on a hook above the poop gutter. Carolyn had already gone to the house, so we turned out the lights and headed for the house. We were sitting down watching TV, and the wife says, "Where's Allen?" We said, "Oh, he's hangin' around down in the barn." She asked a couple times, so we told her what we had done, and oh man, she was mad. She jumped up and headed for the barn, so we decided to go with her. As we got to the barn, we could hear him inside, hollering, "Alright, you guys, I know you're in here. Alright, you guys, I know you're in here. I know you're in here." Momma was not happy when we got him down.

While we were still in Wisconsin, all my boys were into wrestling in school. My oldest boy, William Jay, was a champion wrestler. By the time we were in California, he had already left home and was in the racehorse business. My youngest boy, Allen Wade, wrestled for three years as a ninety-pounder. He was the most valuable wrestler on the team. I told them that if they played sports, they didn't have to come home and do chores. They had an athletic bus that brought them home at night. We drove through some deep snow in Wisconsin to get to some of those wrestling matches. The two youngest boys brought wrestling with them to California. In our spare time, my wife and I would still go square dancing.

My children are my legacy, and I only hope that they can learn from the mistakes I made and that when I am gone, this book will give them and my grandchildren an opportunity to share the great life Carolyn and I had—something I hope every family can share with their children. The Lord has been by my side throughout my life. Sometimes I abandoned him, but he came to my rescue when times were most difficult.

## CHAPTER 12

# MY LIFE, MY WIFE, MY LORD

Many things happened during my lifetime that had a profound effect on me and made me who I am today. Times of happiness and times of sadness. Most are related to my family. My life is really about an old man who left the Lord out of his life until he was nearly dead. That's when I realized God hadn't forgotten me. Basically, life has to be lived day by day and is lived in little bitty intervals. What we're doing is living insignificant days, not planning for the future, and the next thing you know, the future is gone and you're looking at the past.

My daddy was born in 1917, and his mother didn't bother to give him a middle name, so his name was Willis Severs. My mother was born in 1920 or 1921, and her name was Edna Opal Timmons. We're not sure of the date of her birth because her birth certificate was messed up. They were both born in Oxly, Missouri, or somewhere around there. My only brother, Benny Willis Severs, born in 1939, was two years older than me. My only sister, Margerie Ellen Severs, was two years younger than me. My brother and I were both born in a cabin, and my sister was born in a hospital.

When I was a little kid, my daddy taught my brother how to play the guitar. My brother strummed the guitar and played it all the time, and Daddy, he was a fiddler. But Daddy, he could play any stringed instrument. He always made the comment that the only instrument he couldn't play was the harp. I tried to play the banjo and the mandolin. But Daddy was very abusive. He would get to drinking, and my brother, if he wasn't doing something just the way Daddy thought he should with the guitar, Daddy would beat him about the rear end to the point it was pitiful. After I took two or three of those beatings because I wasn't playing the banjo or mandolin the right way, I decided I didn't need any more of that, so I put them away. I never played anything but the radio after that.

I don't recall Daddy ever telling me he loved me. He was the kind of man who would bend over and tap himself on the butt cheek and tell you, "You can kiss me good night here on the cheek." But he never hugged you, never said he loved you.

My daddy died in 1985; he was sixty-eight years old. He died on the operating table during open-heart surgery. He had the same type of problems I've got. The night before Daddy went into the operating room, he called me and told me for the first time that he loved me. I created a sculpture called *Hillbilly Heaven*. It's a cowboy knelt down, and he's playing the harp, and he's got wings. That is a sculpture I made of my daddy. Daddy is now playing the harp.

Carolyn and I have lived everywhere, in seven states and more than twenty different towns over a span of almost eighty years. My sculptures can be found all over the United States, and you can even buy them in Tokyo, Japan. If you had ever told me that my sculptures would be scattered all over the world, I would have never ever believed it. The good Lord has blessed me in so many different ways.

In 1972, my brother, Benny Severs, was killed in a car wreck in Southern Illinois. He left a note saying he was going to take his life. There was road construction going on. A bridge was being rebuilt, and they had taken out the bridge and had a detour exit there. They had barricades up, and my brother drove through the barricades. He never left any kind of skid marks and drove his car right up underneath a tractor trailer that was being used for equipment storage. His car went under at just about windshield height. It practically decapitated him. My brother was thirty-two years old and was having some marital problems. I've often regretted telling him that he married her and should stay with her. I've learned from that experience. Don't ever tell anyone what they should do, because my brother stayed with her, which may have contributed to him killing himself. Sometimes it's best to stay out of other people's business. My brother left behind three little boys, Jerry, Mike, and Ronnie. I've been out of their lives and have very seldom seen them since they were teens. Part of it is my fault, part of it their fault. We just kind of went our own ways.

I want to tell you about my wife's parents. Her daddy, William J. Spangler, was born in Creede, Colorado, in 1903. He lived to be seventy-nine and died of cancer. Her mother, Unice Mary McMann, was born in Clara, Iowa, in 1910. Clara was named after my wife's grandpa, her mother's daddy, who came over from Ireland, and they named the town where he settled after him. I have never been there, but I think it's just a little wide spot in the road. My wife's daddy married when he was young for just one year. He had no children by that marriage. It didn't work out, and he married again at age thirty-eight. He and Unice Spangler had only one child, and that was my wife, Carolyn Saddie Severs.

Just like a horse trainer, Jesus took a rope around my neck, back over my nose, up over my ears, and down my cheeks. And the Lord whispered in my ear. I had to learn different things, and he took the time to work with me and teach me. At times, the Lord would take the rope off my halter and trust me to see what I had learned. But now and then, I would kick up my heels, and he found that I had not yet earned my freedom. Now that I'm older and have learned all that I have learned, the Lord has slipped the rope from my halter and set me free.

As we drive through the open country, all we can see is open range, green grass, and beautiful clouds. We are on our way to another craft show and have just gone through Glorieta, New Mexico, headed toward Las Vegas, New Mexico. All we see is a lot of juniper trees and a beautiful blue sky and puffy white clouds. Ahead of us, we see a herd of buffalo showing us their butts. I can't believe we're out here, four hundred miles from nowhere.

I mentioned Glorieta, New Mexico. Most people are not aware of the Civil War Battle of Glorieta Pass. It was the largest and most divisive battle of the New Mexico campaign. It ended the Confederacy's efforts to capture the territory and other parts of the Western United States. Most of us don't think about the Civil War being fought in the West. The goal of the Confederacy was to gain access to the gold and silver mines of California and the Colorado Territory and the seaports in Southern California and thus evade the Union naval blockade. Glorieta Pass was the turning point of the war for control in the western territories. The dream of a Confederate stronghold in the Southwest was not practical. The Battle of Glorieta Pass was considered a class A battlefield on the same level as Gettysburg and Antietam. Since 1993, it has been part of the National Park Service. Several years ago, to make way for a new highway, several Civil War soldiers' bodies were moved to a new burial site. The amazing thing was when they dug them up to move them, their bodies were mummified. Their uniforms were intact. They were put in new coffins and moved to a new location. They say that the clay dirt and dry climate caused their bodies to be preserved in a mummified condition, kind of like mummies found in ancient Egypt. There's some Civil War history most people don't know about.

We're getting close to Wagon Mound, New Mexico. The grass is green as far as you can see. There is a mountaintop on the edge of the horizon with a blue haze, but not a house in sight. Just rolling hills with juniper trees everywhere. Over to the left, I see a big herd of antelope running on the plains. Tom, I wish you were here with me. Just Carolyn and me celebrating the first day of the rest of our lives. And what a life it has been.

## Carolyn Severs
October 14, 1940–September 4, 2018

## Dewey Severs
April 10, 1941–April 17, 2020

Buried in Mountain View Cemetery,
Moriarty, New Mexico

CHAPTER 13

# DEWEY'S SCULPTURES

*by Tom L. Arnold*

All of Dewey's sculptures start with a vision of what the product will look like and represent something he experienced during his life. The horseshoe is associated with Dewey in his work life as a farrier, a teamster—a driver of teams of horses and mules—and, finally, a renowned sculptor. Each one starts with a horseshoe and then is crafted into a beautiful, lasting shape, all original and one of a kind. The following describes each item's history and origin. Two of the sculptures, *Gail's Hunt* and *Jack Russell*, were created for me, and I have a personal story to share about each of them. This is just a sampling of the hundreds of sculptures Dewey created during his lifetime.

# Horseshoe

Since the early history of domestication of the horse, working animals were exposed to many conditions that created breakage or excessive hoof wear. A horseshoe is a product designed to protect a horse hoof from wear. Shoes are attached on the ground side of the hooves, usually nailed through the insensitive hoof wall that is anatomically similar to the human toenail, although much larger and thicker. The fitting of horseshoes is a professional occupation conducted by a farrier, who specializes in preparing feet, assessing potential lameness issues, and fitting appropriate shoes for horses. In the United States, where licensing is not required, professional organizations provide certification programs that identify qualified individuals.

The earliest written use of horseshoes dates to AD 910. By the thirteenth century, shoes were forged in large quantities and could be bought ready-made. Hot shoeing, the process of shaping a heated horseshoe immediately before placing it on the horse, became common in the sixteenth century. In 1835, the first US patent for a horseshoe manufacturing machine capable of making up to sixty horseshoes per hour was issued to Henry Burden.

Many changes brought about by the domestication of the horse led to a need for shoes for numerous reasons, mostly linked to management resulting in horses' hooves being less hard and more vulnerable to injury. Horses' hooves can become quite worn when subjected to the added weight and stress of a rider, pack load, cart, or wagon. Shoeing, when performed correctly, causes no pain to the animal. Farriers trim the insensitive part of the hoof, which is the same area into which they drive the nails. The farrier uses a rasp, or a large file, to smooth the edge where it meets the shoe and eliminate any sharp edges left from cutting off the nails.

Horseshoes have long been considered lucky. They were originally made of iron, a material that was believed to ward off evil spirits, and traditionally were held in place with seven nails—seven being a lucky number. The superstition acquired a Christian twist due to a legend surrounding the tenth-century saint Dunstan, who worked as a blacksmith before becoming archbishop of Canterbury. The legend recounts that, one day, the devil walked into Dunstan's shop and asked him to shoe his horse. Dunstan pretended not to notice him and agreed to the request; but rather than nailing the shoe to the horse's hoof, he nailed it to the devil's own foot, causing him great pain. Dunstan eventually agreed to remove the shoe, but only after extracting a promise that the devil would never enter a household with a horseshoe nailed to the door. Opinion is divided as to which way up the horseshoe ought to be nailed. Some say the ends should point up so the horseshoe catches the luck. Others say they should point down so the luck is poured upon those entering the home. Superstitious sailors believe that nailing a horseshoe to the mast will help their vessel avoid storms.

A stylized variation of the horseshoe is used for a popular throwing game, horseshoes. The sport involves a horseshoe being thrown as close as possible to a rod to score points. As far as it is known, the sport is as old as horseshoes themselves. While traditional horseshoes can still be used, most organized versions of the game use sport horseshoes, which do not fit on horses' hooves.

## The Cowboy

The term *cowboy* was in use by 1849. Since then, the American cowboy has been romanticized in movies and TV shows. As a child, I can remember my favorite TV shows like *The Lone Ranger*, *Hopalong Cassidy*, *The Roy Rogers and Dale Evans Show*, and many more. As a young kid, I wore my six-shooter—or cap gun—cowboy hat, and boots. A favorite neighborhood game was cowboys and Indians. Beginning in the 1920s and continuing to the present day, Western films popularized the cowboy lifestyle but also formed present stereotypes. In some cases, the cowboy and the violent gunslinger were often associated with one another. Cowboys in movies were often shown fighting with American Indians. Most armed conflicts occurred between native people and cavalry units of the US Army. Relations between cowboys and Native Americans varied but were generally unfriendly. Some of the cowboy movies have immortalized famous Western characters like Billy the Kid, Buffalo Bill, and Jesse James; African American cowboys like Bill Pickett and Nat Love; and Pearl Hart, an American bandit and the Old West's only known female stagecoach robber. Fascination for the cowboy is endless.

The real American cowboy is not as glamorous as his reputation. The average cowboy is an animal herder who tends ranch cattle on horseback and often performs other ranch-related tasks. In addition to ranch work, some cowboys work for or participate in rodeos. The men who drive cattle for a living in the Southwest are usually called cowhands, drovers, or stockmen. The term *cowhand* appeared in about 1852, and *cowpoke* in 1881. *Cowpoke* was originally restricted to the individuals who prodded cattle with long poles to load them onto railroad cars for shipping. Today, *cowboy* is a common term throughout the West and particularly in the Great Plains and Rocky Mountains. Cowboys often began work as adolescents. Historically, cowboys earned wages as soon as they developed sufficient skills to be hired, often as young as twelve or thirteen. With the arrival of railroads in the West, the demand for cowboys increased. They were needed to drive cattle from the ranches where they were raised to the nearest railheads, often hundreds of miles away. American cowboys were drawn from multiple sources.

Following the Civil War and the expansion of the cattle industry, former soldiers from both the Union and the Confederacy came west seeking work, as did large numbers of white men in general. A significant number of African American freedmen also were drawn to the cowboy life, in part because there was not quite as much racial discrimination in the West. A significant number of Mexicans and American Indians already living in the region also worked as cowboys. Today, some Native Americans in the Western United States own cattle and small ranches, and many are employed as cowboys, especially on ranches located near Indian reservations. Also, the Indian cowboy is part of the rodeo circuit.

Regardless of ethnicity, most cowboys came from lower social classes, and the pay was poor. The average cowboy earned approximately a dollar a day, plus food, and, when near the home ranch, a bed in the bunkhouse, usually a barracks-like building with a single open room. Informal competition arose between cowboys seeking to test their cattle- and horse-handling skills against one another, and thus, from the necessary tasks of the working cowboy, the sport of rodeo developed.

Cattle drives transcended hundreds of miles. The route from Texas to the railhead at Abilene, Kansas, became known as the Chisholm Trail. By 1877, the largest of the cattle-shipping boomtowns—Dodge City, Kansas—shipped out five hundred thousand head of cattle. It would take as long as two months to travel from a home ranch to a railhead. The Chisholm Trail was one thousand miles long. By the 1890s, the fencing in of ranch land with barbed wire created the end of the open range. Hence, large cattle drives were over, but smaller cattle drives continued into the 1940s.

The typical attire for a cowboy included a bandanna for mopping up sweat and masking the face from dust storms and chaps for protecting the rider's legs while on horseback. Cowboy boots had high tops to protect the lower legs, pointed toes to help guide the feet into the stirrups, and high heels to keep the feet from slipping through the stirrups while working in the saddle, with or without spurs. A cowboy hat had a wide brim to protect from the sun or hanging brush. Gloves, usually deerskin or other leather, provided protection from barbed wire, assorted tools, or brush and vegetation. And, finally, they wore a good pair of jeans made of canvas or denim. Along with the proper attire, the cowboy carried a lariat, sometimes called a lasso; boot spurs; and usually a firearm, a rifle or a pistol, to protect livestock from wild animals or feral dogs. The traditional means of transport for the cowboy was, of course, by horseback. Horses can travel over terrain that vehicles cannot access. The horse breed of choice was the American quarter horse.

In 2005, the United States Senate declared the fourth Saturday of July as the National Day of the American Cowboy.

## End of the Trail

The *End of the Trail* sculpture is emblematic of the Trail of Tears, the ethnic cleansing and forced displacement of approximately sixty thousand people of the Five Civilized Tribes between 1830 and 1850 by the United States government. Even though the effort was opposed by many, including US Congressman Davy Crockett of Tennessee, then-President Andrew Jackson was able to gain congressional passage of the Indian Removal Act of 1830, which authorized the government to extinguish any Indian claims to land titles in the Southeast. American settlers had been pressuring the federal government to remove Indians from the Southeast, and many settlers had already encroached on Indian lands. As part of the removal, members of the Cherokee, Muscogee or Creek, Seminole, Chickasaw, and Choctaw nations were forcibly removed from their ancestral homelands in the Southeastern United States. These tribes had been living autonomously in the American Deep South. They were relocated to the newly designated Indian Territory west of the Mississippi River after the passage of the Indian Removal Act of 1830. The Cherokee removal in 1838, the last forced removal east of the Mississippi, was brought on by the discovery of gold near Dahlonega, Georgia, in

1828, resulting in the Georgia Gold Rush. The relocated people suffered from exposure, disease, and starvation while en route to their new Indian reserve. Thousands died from disease alone before reaching their destination or shortly after.

The process of cultural transformation from the traditional Indian way of life to the accepted white way of life as proposed by George Washington and Henry Knox was gaining momentum. By 1838, the last group, the Cherokee, were removed; however, a small number were able to evade removal, and they remain in their ancestral homelands today. A number of non-Indians who lived with the nations, including over four thousand slaves and others of African descent such as spouses or freedmen, accompanied the Indians on the trek westward. By 1837, this relocation opened up twenty-five million acres for white settlement.

The forced relocation and ethnic cleansing of the Indian nations has sometimes been referred to as a death march, in particular when referring to the 1838 Cherokee march across Tennessee, Kentucky, and Missouri. Exposure to the elements, disease, starvation, harassment by local frontiersmen, and insufficient rations killed up to one-third of the marchers. This was a dark period in the evolution of the American Southeast and Southwest.

## The Old Windmill

In the eighteenth and nineteenth centuries, the Great Plains were considered unfit for cultivation. The area was termed the Great American Desert. Droughts would follow rainy spells, and the sun and wind would dry up the surface moisture. On the Plains, early settlers could barely haul enough water for personal needs, let alone to grow crops or water livestock. The majority of the water flowed deep underground, often more than three hundred feet below the earth's surface. European windmills were impractical on the American Plains. They were large and expensive and required constant maintenance, as their cloth sails had to be furled by hand.

In 1854, Daniel Halladay developed the American-type windmill. It was smaller and less expensive and could be shipped and built easily. These new windmills were ideal for settlers on the Plains. They could pump water from great depths at a steady rate. They could shift into the prevailing winds and function well in fast and slow winds. Homesteaders, farmers, and ranchers were no longer dependent on natural water, as they could drill wells and pump water. Windmills were often among a homesteader's most prized possessions. The water pumped by windmills was used to cook, bathe, drink, water crops and animals, wash clothes, and more.

Also, railroad development across the western landscape was very dependent on windmills. Steam locomotives had to be watered at regular intervals. On the first transcontinental railroad, windmills had to be placed about every twenty miles to pump water for the trains. Windmills helped speed up western migration. Ranchers could build up herds, farmers planted more, and railroads could pump water into tanks along their routes. The decline of the windmill on the western landscape began after World War I. Electricity and gasoline became cheaper, allowing for alternatives to supply water. The 1936 Rural Electrification Act enabled more farms to have electricity. They could now use electricity to operate electric powered pumps.

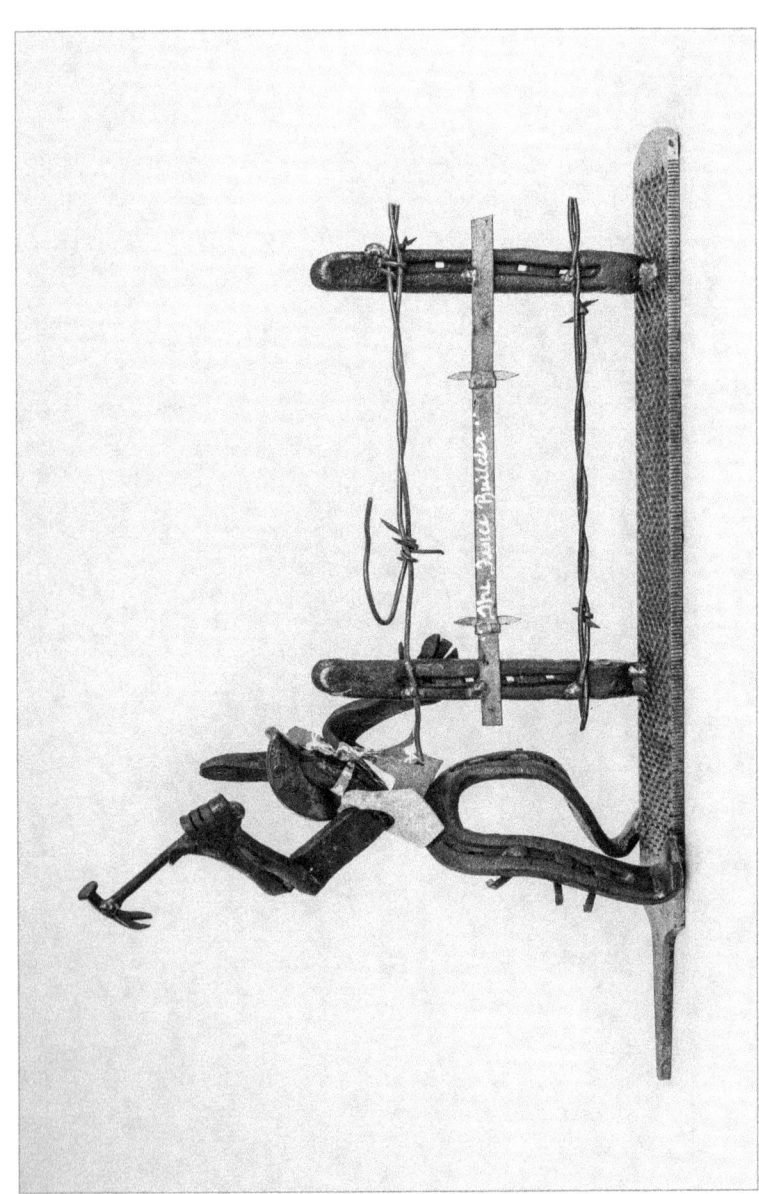

## The Fence Builder

In the Old West, ranchers and settlers needed a way to protect and control their herds as well as maintain their lands—a feat easier said than done until the invention of barbed wire. Before barbed wire, either fences had to be made completely out of wood or hedgerows were planted to make a barrier, but neither provided a viable option in the West. In the settling of the West, one of the greatest challenges was the ability for families to draw boundaries, keeping people, crops, and cattle in—or out. With too few trees to build wooden fences, and walls of prickly vegetation too slow to grow, some enterprising settlers began tinkering with wire; however, there was a major problem. When a wire fence was placed between a thousand-pound Texas longhorn and a bunch of green pasture, it proved to be something of a pushover. That's where the barbs came in. They varied widely, from lines of alternating spikes and wooden boards to sheets of wood studded with spikes. The first barbed wire prototype was called thorny wire. At first, they were all made by hand. In 1874, an Illinois farmer named Joseph Glidden gained a patent for a mechanically produced barbed wire that could be made at scale. Mass production sent homesteaders on a fencing spree.

There was a downside to fencing the West. Law of the open range prevailed. Cowboys drove their cattle to sales; the herd could crisscross the land, drinking water and grazing as they went. Barbed wire restricted cattle's access to streams and rivers. Wire was everywhere. By 1885, the entire Texas panhandle was already fenced. The effect on wildlife was catastrophic. Open-range cattle were deprived of water. Native Americans called barbed wire "devil's rope" because it ensnared wild buffalo. Like cattle, the buffalo struggled to see the thin wire before they were wrapped up in it. Trapped, they often died of hunger or thirst or succumbed to infection as their barbed wounds festered.

Humans weren't exempt from barbed wire's wrath. A company promoting the use of barbed wire advertised it by saying, "Farmers and ranchers can keep out Native Americans, black people, children, beasts owned by others, and poor people with the new invention." It was also promoted for use in prisons, concentration camps, border walls, and areas with unwanted wildlife. Even today, barbed wire's use hasn't changed. In the West, its primary use continues to be fencing in cattle, but it's also used for horses, sheep, goats, llamas, alpacas, and even exotic animals like bison, elk, and deer. Newer innovations have eliminated the barbs, changed the post spacing and two-by-four-inch wire spacing to keep horses' hooves from getting stuck, and increased the strength enough to impede a fifteen-hundred-pound animal. Modern coating methods provide a life span of fifty years. Barbed wire proclaims that you are kept out or in, and, when you resist, it rips you. Other barriers weather, crumble, and grow moss; wire merely rusts and keeps its sting.

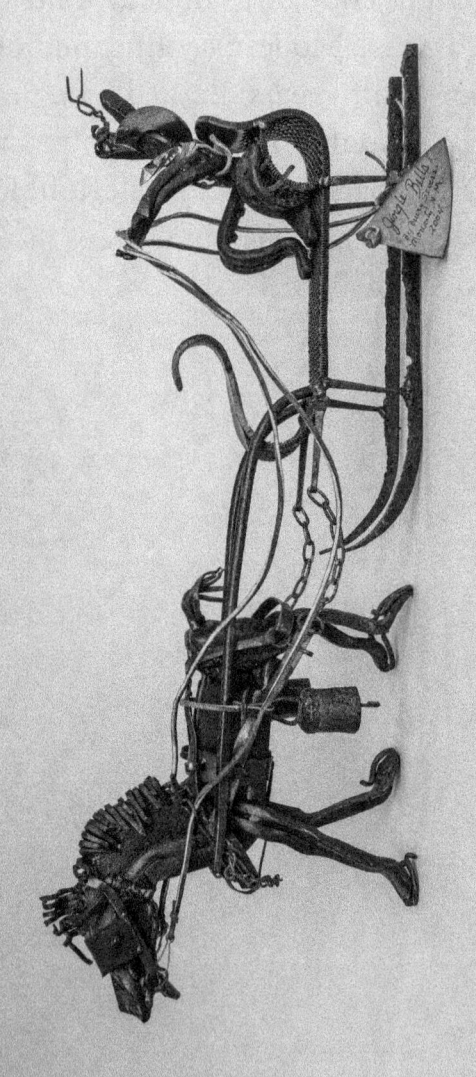

## Jingle Bells

*Dashing through the snow*
*In a one-horse open sleigh*
*O'er the hills we go*
*Laughing all the way*
*Bells on bobtail ring*
*Making spirits bright*
*Oh what sport to ride and sing*
*A sleighing song tonight*

This joyful wintertime tune was originally published in 1857. It's one of the most widely recognized songs in existence. A Christmas hit in the 1940s thanks to Bing Crosby and the Andrews Sisters, the song captures a bygone America in which horses served a central role in everyday life. The jingling bells describe the bells that lined leather harnesses or sleigh shafts of the time. It was the custom—and in some cases, local law—to drive with bells as a precautionary measure. Sled runners glided smoothly over the ground, and snow muffled the sounds of horses, making horse-drawn sleighs a nearly silent form of transportation. As such, clinking bells helped drivers avoid collisions at intersections and alerted passersby to a sled's approach.

Sleighs were used for both chores and revelry before autos made them obsolete. From 1884 until the 1930s, there were frequent references to sleighs or sleighing weather until automobiles and plowed roadways ended what had been standard winter transportation. Sleighs came in many sizes. A horse-drawn sleigh was considered strictly utilitarian, necessary to get around for business, errands, church, or various social events on snow-covered roads. Sleighs had to be brought out of storage when the snow began falling. Studs were needed on horseshoes to get through the snow. It was certainly convenient to do errands or chores, go to church, carry on business, or pay visits by sleigh; however, the roads weren't always snow-covered throughout the winter, due to thaws or sometimes a lack of snow. And then sometimes there could be too much snow, especially if blizzard conditions had piled up high snowdrifts across roads. These weather conditions made sleighs impractical. Sleighs were also used by farmers for taking produce to market or, if they had surplus hay to sell, to the nearest dealer. For most people, a sleigh ride to a social event was greatly anticipated and highly enjoyed. Sleigh rides were great treats for children, both then and today.

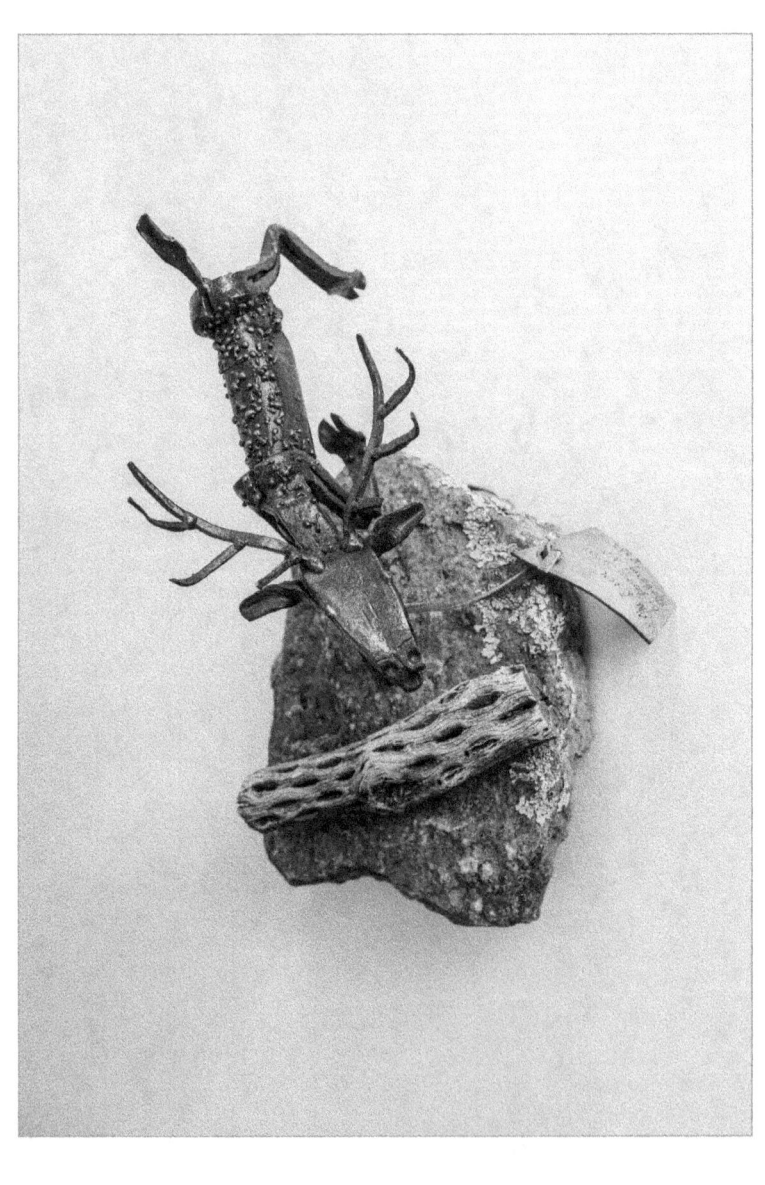

## *The Deer*

A deer is a hoofed ruminant animal. The male is a buck, and the female is a doe. All male deer have antlers. A doe generally has one or two fawns at a time; triplets, while not unknown, are uncommon. Mating season typically begins in late August and lasts until December. Some species mate until early March. The gestation period can be up to ten months. Most fawns are born with their fur covered in white spots, though in many species, they lose these spots by the end of their first winter. In the first twenty minutes of a fawn's life, the fawn begins to take its first steps. The fawn and its mother stay together for about one year. A male usually leaves and never sees his mother again, but females sometimes come back with their own fawns and form small herds. Deer have long had economic significance to humans. Deer meat, known as venison, is highly nutritious. Venison is most often obtained through deer hunting.

Deer hunting is a popular activity in the US that can provide the hunter's family with high-quality meat, and it generates revenue for states and the federal government from the sale of licenses, permits, and tags. The US Fish and Wildlife Service estimates that license sales generate approximately $700 million annually.

However, automobile collisions with deer can impose a significant cost on the economy. In the US, about 1.5 million deer-vehicle collisions occur each year. Accidents cause about 150 human deaths and $1.1 billion in property damage annually. The skins from deer make a strong, soft leather known as buckskin. The hooves and antlers are used for ornamental purposes and for making umbrella handles, knife handles, light fixtures, etc. Deer have become a natural part of the environment for life in rural America.

## Gail's Hunt

I commissioned the *Gail's Hunt* sculpture in honor of my grandfather, Gail "G. T." Arnold. It features a coon—raccoon—poised in the top of a tree, two dogs at the base of the tree baying at the coon, and two coon hunters looking up at the top of the tree, one holding a rifle and the other holding a lantern. The base of the sculpture is a stone native to New Mexico. Some of my fondest memories, beginning at five or six years old through my high school years, are coon hunting with my father and grandfather. We lived in a small town in Northwestern Ohio, and coon hunting was very popular during the 1940s, '50s, and '60s. Raccoon pelts were popular for clothing and provided income as well as a sporting activity. Coon hunting has been around for several centuries.

Coon hunting with dogs is historically the most common method of finding raccoons. Raccoons are nocturnal, so hunting is typically done at night. The place to hunt coon is in a wooded or pasture area with fruit- or nut-bearing trees and a water source nearby. The dogs used for coon hunting are called coonhounds and are known for their ability to trail a scent. There are six coonhound breeds: black-and-tan, redbone, English, bluetick, treeing walker, and Plott. The first breed to be officially registered back in 1900 was the black-and-tan coonhound.

My experience growing up was with the black-and-tan and bluetick breeds. Hunting at night, we would turn the dogs loose, and they would trail and chase the raccoon up a tree. Once the raccoon was in the tree with the dogs at the base, it was referred to as "treed." The most difficult part of training a coon dog to trail and tree is teaching the dog to hunt raccoons and ignore other animals, such as opossums, deer, and rabbits. The dogs are released at night in an area where raccoons are likely to be—such as woods, crop fields, or creek banks—and allowed to find a scent. Most dogs will emit a long, distinct bay upon striking a trail and will continue to bay the entire time they are tracking the raccoon. The hunt typically ends when the raccoon climbs a tree. Upon reaching the tree, the dog or dogs will stop baying and begin the tree bark, also referred to as the chop bark for its short, sharp sound. This change in vocalization lets the hunter know when a raccoon has been treed. The hunter may either follow the dog or remain in one place and only go after the dog once it has treed the raccoon.

We usually followed the dogs carrying a kerosene lantern, and once we arrived at the treed coon, we used a strong flashlight to find the coon in the tree. We wore boots to cross creeks and manage mud and rough terrain. To shoot the coon from the tree, a .22 rifle was preferred. The preferred gun for my grandfather was a Marble Game Getter, called an over-and-under, which was a combination .22-caliber rifle and .410 shotgun. It was lightweight with a collapsible handle and a leather holster for carrying. Killing raccoons is legal during a specified hunting season, usually September to February.

Raccoons were first hunted by Native Americans, who harvested them for meat and fur. George Washington is credited with owning some of the first coon-hunting dogs. In 1885, a raccoon pelt sold for twenty-five cents. In the 1970s, the price was as high as twenty-five to thirty dollars each. It was possible to catch ten raccoons per night with good dogs. Raccoon fur coats were a fashion trend in the 1920s, leading to high pelt prices and an increase in hunting and trapping. During the Great Depression of the 1930s, when many rural families lived in poverty, raccoons were hunted extensively and became relatively rare. Hunters sold pelts for needed money, and the meat provided protein. Even with no market for raccoon pelts today, coon hunting is still enjoyed.

## Jack Russell

Many years ago, during a ten-year period in my life, my obsession and hobby was training and competing with my Jack Russell terriers. Over that period, I traveled to several southern and midwestern states and Canada several times a year to compete, sometimes as often as two weekends a month. Two of my dogs, Dixie (1998–2017) and Rusty (1996–2012), won numerous championships in several events, including racing, go-to-ground, agility, and lure coursing. Dixie was a two-time Canadian national racing champion and the second-fastest dog in the US. Rusty was a Canadian national agility champion, won many regional go-to-ground championships, and participated in an Animal Planet TV series named *The Superstar Challenge*, filmed at Universal Studios in Orlando, Florida. Rusty also filmed TV commercials and was the halftime show in two professional soccer matches, showing off his ball-handling skills and goal scoring.

The Jack Russell terrier was first bred by Reverend John "Jack" Russell in England around 1850. They were bred to bolt foxes out of their burrows. They have high stamina for the hunt as well as the courage to chase out prey that have gone underground. They were used for foxhunting in the

United States in the early nineteenth century. Jack Russells have appeared in films, television, and print. Nipper, born in 1884, became the famous RCA Victor dog. Other famous Jack Russells include Soccer, of the TV series *Wishbone*, and Moose and his son Enzo, who played the role of Eddie on the TV sitcom *Frasier*. Most recently, a dog named Patron learned how to sniff out Russian explosives in Ukraine and located over ninety explosives, saving numerous lives.

Jack Russell terriers come in a variety of coat types and a range of markings. They must be at least 51 percent white with black, brown, or tan. They are extremely intelligent, athletic, fearless, and vocal. If not properly stimulated and exercised, they can become moody or destructive. My favorite event is racing, the most exciting of all terrier trial events. There are two types of races—flat and hurdle. The typical track is 150 to 200 feet long, with a starting box at one end and a catching area at the other end. The dogs chase a lure, usually a piece of scented fur, that is pulled ahead of them for the length of the track. The dogs are muzzled for their safety.

Dewey created this sculpture for me of a dog going over a hurdle—as a reminder of many wonderful trials with my dogs.

CHAPTER 14

# DEWEY'S POEMS

I was sixty-three years old when I began to write poetry. I was short on faith, but I still found time to sit and talk to God every day of the week. It was my way of worshipping and praising God. I would sit and talk to him as I wrote poems. I made up the words like I was singing to the Lord, and they became poems. My poetry is nothing more than moments of love, anger, and despair. It comes from deep down inside of me. There are so many things that inspire me to write poetry. I can't sing, so I think about writing poems as I beat on the anvil, making sculptures. The Lord gives me the words, and I just write them down. They are mostly about me, my wife, and my father in heaven. I also wrote some about my children. I have written over sixty poems telling people about Jesus.

> When all starts
> to fall apart
> and look bad,
>
> remember all
> them blessin's
> you done had.
>
> Never did I see
> a good crop
> grow
>
> 'less there
> was some weeds
> ya had to hoe.

## *Why Did He Do What He Done*

Did ya ever stop and think why God did what he done?
He gave us ten commandments, knowing we couldn't keep none.

Now why would someone with so much power be so mean as to make us want to cower?

He told us if'n we failed in any way,
if'n we even thought we'd die someday.

He loosed the devil like a roaring lion with our souls to play.
Then he gave us all these rules and told us in these boundaries we must stay.

Why, when he says he loves us so much,
did he put so much evil around us to touch?

Why does evil glitter and shine and try to lure us?
How could he be such an ornery old cuss?

He told us thru faith we must trust in someone we can't even see.
He said that one would come who had not sinned in any way. How can that be?

He gave Abraham an only son and then
told him to sacrifice him.
He'd live on thru that line, he said.
How could that be if'n his son were dead?

Now the Bible says we're all created
equal, but some he gives all the wealth.
Others, I don't understand why, but they
got nuttin' but poor health.

Now I ain't too smart, but this don't seem fair,
when others got everything, not even a care.

Even the profit Moses left wandering in
the desert for forty years.
And then when he'd finally found the land,
he told him he couldn't enter it;
he could only see it thru his tears.

Why did he have Noah spend so many
years gatherin' animals and building an
ark with his hands,
when all he had to do was just leave one
little piece of dry land?

Now you tell me why he put Adam to sleep
and took one of his ribs
and then allowed Eve to go and do what she did.

*Tom L. Arnold*

Now they say the pathway up is really
narrow and only a few can find.
But then he paved a road down, and it's all
streamlined.

Now I wouldn't think this problem would
take no mastermind.
All ya gotta do at the gate to heaven is
put up a slow movin' sign.

Now I know he has showed us a lot of love,
but I'm here to tell ya I got a lot of
questions for above.

Ya see, I'm just an old man, so confused I am
'bout God and the devil and all his great plan.

He gave us Christ, his very own son,
knowing most would not listen
but he'd still save some.

I reckon he did what he done
'cause he knew someday we'd realize
we needed the savior, his son.

## The Trail Boss

This were a mighty mean critter, and the ground
done shook, and it became somewhat dark.
He done rode this hea critter as it reached for
the sky. Its hide seemed tough as bark.

Now he done rode this critter alls by hisself,
no hat, chaps, nor spurs.
Seems whiles he rode, two other fellers were
a'ridin' next to him, and one was shoutin' slurs.

He done stuck like glue, ya could even say
he seemed nailed ta this hea steed.
Somehow his side done got pierced, and they
all watched him bleed.

The clouds rumbled, and this feller's hair
danced in the wind.
He done rode this critter thru the gates of
hell to free us of our sin.

His compadres didn't even stick to see his ride,
but he forgave them and took it all in stride.
When it was over, they had to lift him down
lengthwise.
He was so all in, it took three days afore he
could rise.

Now they say he went to repair fences and fix up
the bunkhouse on his spread; he had some
holes to dig.
He said to watch the horizon, fer someday
soon he's
a'gonna whistle fer us to come to his big shindig.

I cain't believes it, but they say he runs sheeps
amongst all his cows
and his hosses all drinks and eats
in the very same corrals.

Now I bent down low and asked him who was
this gent
that was so game.
He whispered back real weak that Jesus Christ
were his name.

*The following poem is a true story about a wreck up on a mountain near Eureka, California, with a six-horse hitch. I turned it into a spiritual poem, but it was a true happening near the California redwoods along the coast, close to the Oregon line. It's about three or four thousand cowboys getting together for a big party for days.*

---

### Offerin' Up the Sacrifice

Now I done tolt ya I ain't no cowboy poet;
this ain't no yarn.
This is how God sometimes keeps idiots
and darn folks from harm.

We was on a Sonoma County trailblazers ride.
This was fer real men—no women nor kids;
ya had to be set on suicide.

Ole Louie Silva, he lived in Southern
California, and he kinda screened the
wagons and teams that were to attend.
He wanted teamsters and wagons that
were tough and someswhat salty
that would stick to the bitter end.

There was three, maybe four, thousand
cowboys, pickups, hoss trailers, and such.
It would take five days and nights ta bond.
There was only three wagons with
six-hoss teams tethered ta picket lines.
Dr. Alley and me, his teamster, were one.

Andy Amsbaugh—another six-up
Belgian hitch—done pulled the startin'
gate at Santa Anita racetrack.
Now they had to be mighty quick
ta get all this done for them race
hosses and jockeys ta all get back.

Now ole Louie, he was thin, and his
face were cracked—he were bent from
many, many years.
Andy, he weighed in around two-sixty.
His face were whiskered, and his nose was
red from all those beers.

Now ole Andy was nigh onto eighty
years old and weren't much on spit
and polish.
He'd been around nearly a century, and
he didn't listen ta others; sometimes he
was ornery an' downright bullish.

The six-horse hitches were used fer
carrying beer, pop, whiskey, and such on ice,
but mainly they was there ta offer up
ta God as a sacrifice.

Ya see, the trails were long, narrow,
dusty, and darn steep.
There was one- ta two-hundred-foot
drop-offs and hairpin curves—it'd
make your spine creep.

At times—yer team a'being nearly
thirty-six foot long—yer leaders were done
out of sight.
We kept a rough lock on the side
nearest the bank; if'n the wagon
got close to the edge, it were a fright.

Has ya done ever bit into a persimmon
that was someswhat green?
A'lookin' out over them drop-offs'll
make your butt pucker from what's
ya done seen.

When ya topped a steep incline, about
four or five cowboys tied on dallying
ta the horn.

Tom L. Arnold

This kept the wagon from applying too
much weight ta the britchen, in case
something was worn.

We topped the last steep ridge, and it was
about thirty percent slantin' 'dicular
all the way to the camp.
Andy said, "Nah, I don't need no hep, just
a rough lock, no dally"—he got overconfident.

Now in those days, I was still someswhat
wet behind the ears.
Dr. Alley, my boss, and I looked out
over the precipice with great fear.

Ole Andy said, "Giddyup," and he made six
or eight foot—then the equine defecation
hit the fan.
Da rough lock got off the trail in
the green grass, which weren't in his plan.

At this kind of grade, it was kinda
similar to ice.
You could tell this were the first wagon
offered up fer sacrifice.

Brit McLin raced to the right-hand leader
like old Roy Rogers.

Da bridle was gone, and ole Buck, he
weren't interested in no corn dodgers.

So McLin, he just stayed in his saddle
and turned 'em with his loop.
He know'd after a half mile or so
they was a'runnin' out of poop.

Da wagon was a'given purty good
clip when the front wheel caught a
rock. With one hell of a bounce,
ole Andy toppled from the seat,
stretched across the doubletree,
clutchin' the lines with ever' bounce.

He was strainin' into the moving wheels
with great fear.
His swamper were grabbin' fer the lines
that Andy wouldn't release—as he
screamed into his ear.

The swamper, from the looks, was
a'makin' last minute notes in the flight
recorder.
Ole Andy's face were blank as he
recollected his years—he were a'puttin'
his life in order.

Hoss shoes were snatchin' up grass, dirt,
and dust—sparks flew from rocks
amongst splinters and debris; we
feared it would combust.

Snot, froth, and slobbers was drippin'
from the team's heavin' sides.
From the looks of their bulgin' eyes,
they know'd this weren't no hayride.

The wagon was a'holdin' up darn good
with broken bolsters, cracked reach,
and no seat.
Alley and I know'd—a'bein' next—it
was a'gonna be darn hard fer us
ta still compete.

Ole Buck, he weren't no dummy—he'd
earned the right to lead.
He know'd the sound of the gate at
Anita, and he done cranked up the speed.

Da wagon made the turn, barely
on two wheels.
The beer, pop, and whiskey—she all
began ta unseal.

She rolled over maybe two or three
times, like a lamb at the slaughter.
For she came to a stop;
the sacrifice was complete. Here it
all laid on the altar—which were
a mountaintop.

It was a god-awful sight—all them
cowboys slashin' harnesses with their
knives—and some a'holdin' a head.
Da wagon was on ole Andy, but no
hurry—he surely must be dead.

Da team was stacked in a pile—nuttin'
but harnesses, buttholes, and tails.
Da wagon was upside down on top a'
the swamper and driver. She'd
surely derailed.

Now Andy started squawkin', "I needs
some hep down hea—confounded
artificial hips of mine done popped out."
Thirty-some hands lifted the wagon,
and they dragged ole Andy out.
He hurt so bad, he cuffed one or two
and gave another clout.

Ever'body was a'lookin' fer the
swamper. He was ok, 'cept fer cuts
and bruises; he'd done jumped out.
He were thinkin' about a change—
thot he'd buy a hoss and be a scout.

They suspended ole Andy from the neck
yoke on the tongue.
He jiggled around, cursed a lot, popped
his hips back in whiles he sung.

They set ole Andy on the tailgate of
a pickup, whiles he began to moan.
They braced him up with two or
three shots of Jim Beam—whiles they
loaded da pieces he still owned.

Now the moral of this hea story is—
if'n yer an idiot or moron—don't
put God to the test.
You may find yerself and all yer
belongin's someswhat unblessed.

# ACKNOWLEDGMENTS

Writing this book was a labor of love and took place over twenty years. The inspiration and encouragement came from many sources. The content of the book started with my meeting Dewey in Raleigh, North Carolina, in November 2003. A trip to his home in Moriarty, New Mexico, in June 2004 resulted in many hours of recording his life story with him and his wife, Carolyn. Subsequent phone calls, faxes, and written correspondence with Dewey and Carolyn helped me document his life. Additional credit goes to their son Dewey Lee and his wife, Kelly, for their recent help in verifying names, dates, and events.

Also, I want to remember my close friend Tim Brewer, who was originally going to be my coauthor but was tragically killed in an automobile accident. Most of all, my deceased life partner, Heidi Fletcher, who made sure I fulfilled my promise to complete the book. Thanks also to my friend Alice Chumbley Lora for editing, P. Rae Staton for studio photography, good friend Terry Chappell for creative assistance, and my publisher, Luminare Press.

—Tom L. Arnold

# REFERENCES

Authenticating historical events and background narrative for the book is attributed to the following sources:

"Barbed Wire." n.d. National Cowboy & Western Heritage Museum. Accessed March 5, 2024. https://nationalcowboymuseum.org/explore/barbed-wire/#:~:text=Before%20barbed%20wire%2C%20fences%20had,what%20is%20more%20recognized%20today

"Battle of Glorieta Pass." 2024. Wikipedia, the Free Encyclopedia. Last modified February 21, 2024. https://en.wikipedia.org/wiki/Battle_of_Glorieta_Pass

"Big Thompson River." 2024. Wikipedia, the Free Encyclopedia. Last modified January 20, 2024. https://en.wikipedia.org/wiki/Big_Thompson_River

"Coon Hunting." 2023. Wikipedia, the Free Encyclopedia. Last modified December 15, 2023. https://en.wikipedia.org/wiki/Coon_hunting

"Coon Hunting: The Complete Guide." 2020. Outrigger Outdoors. Last modified September 30, 2020. https://outriggeroutdoors.com/blogs/night-hunting/coon-hunting-the-complete-guide

"Cowboy." 2024. Wikipedia, the Free Encyclopedia. Last modified February 14, 2024. https://en.wikipedia.org/wiki/Cowboy

"Deer." 2024. Wikipedia, the Free Encyclopedia. Last modified February 20, 2024. https://en.wikipedia.org/wiki/Deer

"Doniphan, Missouri." 2024. Wikipedia, the Free Encyclopedia. Last modified February 4, 2024. https://en.wikipedia.org/wiki/Doniphan,_Missouri

Garrison, Robert. 2022. "Remembering the 1976 Big Thompson Canyon Flood." Denver7. Last modified November 8, 2023. https://www.denver7.com/news/local-news/remembering-the-1976-big-thompson-flood

"Horseshoe." 2024. Wikipedia, the Free Encyclopedia. Last modified January 20, 2024. https://en.wikipedia.org/wiki/Horseshoe

"Jack Russell Terrier." 2024. Wikipedia, the Free Encyclopedia. Last modified March 2, 2024. https://en.wikipedia.org/wiki/Jack_Russell_Terrier

"Jack Russell Terrier Racing." n.d. Jack Russell Terrier Club of America. Accessed March 5, 2024. https://www.therealjackrussell.com/trial/racing.php

Johnson, Mary Ellen. 2019. "Sleighs Were Used for Both Chores and Revelry Before Autos Made Them Obsolete." *The Altamont Enterprise*. Last modified December 11, 2019. https://altamontenterprise.com/opinion/columns/glimpse-guilderland-history/12112019/sleighs-were-used-both-chores-and-revelry-autos

"Oxly, Missouri." 2023. Wikipedia, the Free Encyclopedia. Last modified March 30, 2023. https://en.wikipedia.org/wiki/Oxly,_Missouri

Robert. 2021. "A Beginner's Guide to Raccoon Hunting." Eating the Wild. Last modified July 2, 2021. https://eatingthewild.com/a-beginners-guide-to-coon-hunting/

Schnurr, Ryan. 2018. "The Iconic Windmills That Made the American West." Atlas Obscura. Last modified January 15, 2018. https://www.atlasobscura.com/articles/windmills-water-pumping-museum-indiana

Severs, Dewey. "Horseshoe Dreams." *Guideposts*, March 2008.

"Sundown Town." 2024. Wikipedia, the Free Encyclopedia. Last modified February 25, 2024. https://en.wikipedia.org/wiki/Sundown_town

"Trail of Tears." 2024. Wikipedia, the Free Encyclopedia. Last modified February 29, 2024. https://en.wikipedia.org/wiki/Trail_of_Tears

"Windmills on the American Plains." n.d. National Park Service. Accessed March 5, 2024. https://www.nps.gov/articles/windmills

**In Loving Memory**

**Heidi Fletcher**
February 12, 1970–January 26, 2022

www.ingramcontent.com/pod-product-compliance
Lightning Source LLC
LaVergne TN
LVHW010217070526
838199LV00062B/4630